HOW TO MARKET
YOUR PRIVATE INVESTIGATION BUSINESS:
LESS THAN 5 HOURS A WEEK, REALLY!

John A Hoda

CLI, CFE

How To Market Your Private Investigation Business: Less Than 5 Hours A Week, Really!

Copyright John A. Hoda (2019)

All rights reserved. No part of this publication may be reproduced, stored in a retrieval system, or transmitted in any form or by any means with the prior written permission of the publisher.

ISBN: 978-0-9890201-5-2

Requests to publish work from this book should be sent to john@johnhoda.com.

Cover and Interior Illustrations, Titling, and Interior Layout: Creative Jay (creativejay.com)

HOW TO
MARKET
YOUR
PRIVATE INVESTIGATION
BUSINESS

LESS THAN 5 HOURS A WEEK, REALLY!

John A Hoda
CLI, CFE

INTRODUCTION

JOHN A. HODA

The idea behind this book follows this simple axiom: The diet you do is better than the diet you should do, but don't. The exercise you do is better than the exercise you should do but don't.

The marketing that you do is better than the marketing you should do but don't.

It is as much about mindset as it is about action. If you have been resistant to marketing, it's time to change. There's no way out but through. By starting this book, you have shown that you are open to changing your mindset.

Should you market more than 5 hours a week? Probably. Should you have multiple marketing streams? Yup. Spend more money on the marketing plan that has a proven track record? You betcha.

Here's the straight truth. Most Private Investigators spend very little time and money on marketing their private investigations business. They fall into the same trap as other professionals, such as lawyers and doctors. They think that if they put out a superior product (i.e., an exceptional service), the customers will beat down their doors.

INTRODUCTION

Don't get me wrong. There is a value to word-of-mouth marketing. We will talk about testimonials and referrals and how to attract and leverage them later.

The brutal truth of the matter is that, according to some estimates, 85% of all private investigators will throw out their pretty embossed business cards and tri-fold brochures within two years. There are many reasons for that, but one of the biggest ones is they did not attract enough good-paying customers often enough to pay their bills.

There are many books written on sales and marketing. You can spend hours online or in the bookstore looking and searching (though the book that saved my business 16 years ago was sitting next to the counter in a spinner display at a Kinko's where I was getting flyers). I won't denigrate those learning opportunities, but maybe a book written by a still-active private investigator who had to learn about marketing a **Private Investigation Business** might be more focused. The techniques taught here are not a one-size-fits-all approach to business. You won't get marketing advice for pest control or a pizza shop here.

I want to impart some of my hard-earned lessons here, but it will not be a typical "do as I did" manual. I have created two fictional characters to join you on your journey. I want to cover the spectrum of business models of Business-to-Business (B2B) and Business-to-Consumer (B2C) and introduce a concept I think I coined the phrase for, Professional-to-Professional (P2P). There are two types of hybrids that we will talk about as well. The first is the hybrid with such a specialized niche that their specialty crosses all customer groups. Locating people and Skip Tracing come to mind. Then there is the hybrid who lives and works in remote places. Why I didn't hang out a shingle in the Virgin Islands is a mystery to me. Need to find records or do interviews in Eastern Washington State or Montana? Slim Pickings is your guy. When you are the only game in town, you can attract Consumers, Businesses, or Professionals.

First, I want to introduce you to Tony Russo. He retired from the New York City Police Department as a Detective Sergeant. He's working mostly in Queens, NY and eastern Long Island.

Then there is Beth Clark. She's a two-tour veteran of the United States Army with experience in Intelligence from her days in the sandbox of Afghanistan. She relocated to Austin Texas. A single woman of color, she is looking to use her smarts and go into business for herself. She wants to see what she can do without having to deal with the layers of management or bureaucracy between her and the customer. She is building a business selling to the consumer public with the intent that the daily operations will eventually run without her.

Finally, there is my own story following my September 1997 launch date. I was looking to create a business to serve Property & Casualty insurance companies. My goal was to sell my business to my employees and retire wealthy and early.

Suffice it to say you will get many ideas to try out here. Some will fit and some won't; some will stick, some won't. However, in the end, by marketing 5 hours a week through good weeks and bad, you will find what works for you and see the results. There is no short-cut to running a successful PI business, but I am hoping to make your path to the success you deserve straighter and smoother.

DISCLAIMER

PLEASE READ

I have done my best to give you useful and accurate information in this book, but I cannot guarantee that the information is correct or will be appropriate for your particular situation. Law, procedures, and regulations change frequently and are subject to differing interpretations. It is your responsibility to verify all the information and the laws discussed in this book before relying on them. Noting in this book can substitute for legal advice and cannot be considered as making it unnecessary to obtain such advice. In all situations involving local, state and federal law, especially as it relates to PI regulations and carrying weapons, receive specific information from the appropriate government agency.

OVERVIEW OF THIS BOOK

WHAT TO EXPECT

SECTION ONE: The HoneyMoon Is Over (Page 11)
- Six Months To Two Years After Launch
- Examples From Our Characters
- Reasons Why Sales Go Flat
- Marketing Plan Revisited
- Checklist
- Why
- How
- What
- Target Audience
- Pricing
- Services
- SMART Goals
- Competition

Section Two: Keeping Score (Page 31)
- Paragraph
- Time Management
- Critical Items First Thing In The Morning.
- Crm For B2C, B2C, P2P
- Saturday Morning Projects
- Old-Fashioned Flip Chart

Section Three: Branding (Page 47)
- What Does Your Website Really Say?
- What Does Your Collateral Really Say?

Section Four: Targeting The Right Audience (Page 67)
- General V Specific
- User Versus Buyer
- Go Wide Or Go Deep
- Examples Of Targeted Audiences
- Summary
- Checklist

Section Five: Guess What? You Are Always Closing. (Page 85)
- Basics Of Selling AIDA
- Selling Steps
- Example
- Resources

Section Six: When You Are A Hammer, You Are Always In Search Of Nails (Page 109)
- What I Learned From The Parachute
- Examples Of Transferrable Skill Sets.
- "I Don't Do That."
- Refer It Or Learn It
- Beware Bright Shiny Objects
- Beth's Side Hustle
- Summary

Section Seven: You Can Market Less Than 5 Hours A Week. Really! (Page 127)
- Why Less Than 5 Hours A Week?
- Examples Of 5 Hour Marketing Habits
- Your Plan

Section Eight: Flying Fortress (Page 141)
- Conclusion

OVERVIEW OF THIS BOOK

SECTION ONE:
THE HONEYMOON IS OVER

DON'T GET SWALLOWED UP IN YOUR SUCCESS

After you launch your business, regardless of whether it is a soft or a hard launch, you can get swallowed up in minutiae of your own success. You might take on a weekend case for a new customer, or offer a discount to someone that could give you more work or a great testimonial or both. You might be swamped with the fulfillment part of the business (services), all the while thinking, *this is great!*

You don't realize how much time it takes to log a case in, set it up, work it, report on it and bill it, enter it into your accounting software, receive payment, make the deposit, and close the file. You might be taking on new work that requires slightly different skill sets that has a steep learning curve.

Back in the day when you were mining someone else's gold, you might not have returned to a faraway location until the next time you were out there in the hinterlands. Now, you make special trips just to impress your new customers.

It's fun, it's new, and it's exciting. You are building up the checkbook. You are paying your bills. Your family and friends are impressed. You pinch yourself. *Is this real?*

SECTION ONE: THE HONEYMOON IS OVER

Then reality sets in. You bust your butt to get that impossible video shot of Mr. Smith and Mrs. Jones who have a thing going on. You send in the video with your bill, and the client complains that the video is jiggly. You patiently explain the difficulty of obtaining the shot, but you can't get them to understand that this is not Hollywood. The client wants to negotiate your bill—*the nerve.*

Your virus software didn't catch the latest attack from those zany guys in Eastern Europe and you are staring at tons of work to be input, and at least 2 days of having to re-enter data because you thought you were backing up to the cloud, only to find out, unfortunately, that you never tested your back-up plan.

The associate who was scheduled to work with you tomorrow calls you at the last minute, while you are staring at the blue screen of death, and says they can't work with you. You hang up the phone muttering and cursing that ten-year-old nephew of your associate who had to have a birthday party on the same day as your big case.

You have more unplanned work. You have to cancel the big case or throw another warm body at it and to add insult to injury, you notice that you haven't received a new case in a while. You were so mired in fulfillment and the business of your business, you failed to notice that by the end of next week, you will hear crickets when the work dries up. It's then when you slam the new desk drawer closed (and it breaks) you realize the honeymoon is over.

I am about to tell you how Private Investigation marketing is really done. Raise your hand if this applies to you:

- You market when you run out of work.
- You take all comers.
- You discount pricing to keep people on the payroll.
- You wait until after you do everything else, including taking out the trash, before you lift up a phone and dial a prospect.

- Alternatively, follow-up with that prospect from the other day, oops it was last week, ugh no, it was two weeks ago. *Fat chance for that one, bunky!*
- It's been a long day, and you're tired. The launch adrenaline has worn off. The long nights and days have caught up with you.
- *I'll do it tomorrow,* you say. But you don't.
- You don't have a plan.
- You haven't done any marketing in a while, and it feels awkward trying to ask for business again.
- You had gotten so busy you turned off the Live Chat button on your website.
- You haven't put up the new video testimonial that is just sitting there waiting to be uploaded.

Let's check in with Tony, Beth, and John

Russo & Associates has gotten off to a good start. He is hitting his numbers from day one thanks to a soft launch where he used his unused vacation time and comp time to work on cases and go to Chamber of Commerce Leads Groups and BNI meetings. A former District Attorney that he knows invites him to a bar association meeting and introduces him around. All of this leads to coffee or lunches with prospects. At first, he is nervous talking to people about his business, but he learns to shift the conversation to their needs, and how their needs are not being met or not being met satisfactorily. Tony is six months into his new gig.

SECTION ONE: THE HONEYMOON IS OVER

He and his wife are still adjusting to his working at home. Yes, he could put the clothes in the dryer after his marketing calls, no he wasn't vacuuming the stairs on a workday. He likes taking a case in and working it quickly to the happy surprise of his clients who have never received such royal treatment. His bills are fair, and when the first payment checks arrive at his post office box, he feels like a kid a Christmas. He photocopies the first one and frames it, placing it on the same wall as his commendations and awards.

He takes the time to learn how to do his bookkeeping, and his accountant is pleased with his effort. Tony sets aside enough money for taxes and tightens his belt on personal expenses for a while. He can start paying down credit card balances faster than expected. This lifestyle business of P2P resonates with him. The hours are not killer, but he has been warned there will be some adjustments to being the chef, cook, and bottle-washer.

The marketing is still hard to accept. The lure of doing the work is higher than the diligence of marketing, even if only for a little while each day. He tricks himself into thinking that if he gets up early and goes out on his cases, it will create more billable investigative hours.

However, by watching the numbers, he sees his numbers are actually flattening out. He looks at the stack of business cards on his desk. These were people he met, but he got too busy and hadn't bothered to put them into his CRM and follow-up. *Was it too late to call them? Did he fail to strike while the iron was hot? He looked at his watch. 4:30 pm: no, it is too late in the day. He'll call in the morning.* His friend, the former DA, has a case that he wants to talk to Tony about. He will call first thing.

Note: Tony will find out that, in some businesses, calling after the receptionist has gone home means he can leave a message directly on the prospect's voicemail. This generates more return calls than if he had gotten the receptionist in the first place. Provided it is the right message, of course.

Truth Be Told Investigations, Inc. is celebrating its first year in business. Beth Clark and her senior (and only) investigator Mary Chambers are at their favorite taco joint in Austin, Texas. Billy White, their wunderkind IT guy, working on his third beer, is enjoying the music and the cool evening breeze at a picnic table with his two favorite private investigators.

It was this exact spot where Beth had originally drawn up the idea of her business. *Her business!* It was here she was fortunate to have met some of the good folks at App Sumo who recommended Billy to help build out her website. App Sumo understands e-commerce for small business, and there was a chance for Beth to apply their know-how to Private Investigations. So naturally, it is at this taco stand they celebrate. Beth and Mary flip a coin to see who will drive Billy to his apartment—his car will stay there tonight, at the rate he is going.

The numbers are amazing. Working nights and weekends on her armored guard job and the opposite of Mary, cherry-picked from the same company, they can quickly roll out their B2C fidelity and personal private investigations to Austin's upscale community. Her website is SEO optimized. She keeps the leads clicking through the site with video testimonials and a free checklist. Capturing their email with free reports, she converts those leads to prospects.

As important is the website's Live Chat function. Beth and Mary take shifts fielding those calls. Billy made it so easy for them to convert the prospects into customers with the terms of an agreement (contract) baked into the credit card or Paypal payment options on the shopping cart page.

SECTION ONE: THE HONEYMOON IS OVER

Beth attacks the market with reasonably-priced 4-hour or 8-hour flat rates, but what is really eye-popping is the up-sell to use her intelligence skills and OSINT (Open Source Intelligence) to throw more ammo at the target. She raises the price of that up-sell to nearly triple its introductory rate and buyers do not even blink an eye.

These are giddy times, but she knows that her business has to grow substantially if she is to move out of fulfillment and marketing. She doesn't mind that the number of assignments is slowing down. Both she and Mary are getting stricter in taking on new clients from their Live Chats. They do not fully listen to the opportunities people come to them with. If the cases don't fit into the easy to digest flat rates, they pass on them. *They are passing on potentially more significant and long-time hourly assignments they could work and fit into their schedule.* This is nagging Beth but doesn't bother Mary whatsoever. Mary didn't have an equity stake in the business and wants to work the 4-hour cases because they are easier. Tonight, however, they will celebrate.

DON'T GET SWALLOWED UP IN YOUR SUCCESS

John was turning green from the Cuban cigar he was smoking outside of the Toronto hotel where the International Association of Special Investigation Units was holding its annual conference in 1998. It was almost a year to the day that he started Independent Special Investigations, LLC. His employees, Jon and Chris, were there with his soon-to-be surveillance manager Frank. They were all wearing identical white polos with the ISI logo embroidery. They were the only private investigators attending the conference.

Yes, they had business cards and brochures, but no booth. The conversations with the other attendees were amiable and not focused. Qualify prospects? What's that you say? His company provided Insurance Fraud Investigations to this exact group. Everyone in attendance was a prospect. He tended to saddle up to the bar with other investigators and didn't ask for an introduction to their supervisors in attendance. He talked about being in southern New England but didn't emphasize being able to work in New York City at all. Attendees didn't know what John's Unique Selling Proposition (USP) was. John picked up a few business cards and didn't follow up on any of them.

They were there for the training, or so he thought. He went to a Toronto Blue Jays baseball game with some of the directors of the association and didn't introduce himself, same for a tour of the Space Needle. He had more work than he could handle and would be adding two more investigators in the next six months and a surveillance group under Frank's guidance. What did he have to market for?

SECTION ONE: THE HONEYMOON IS OVER

What a missed opportunity!

John, in the months leading up to his launch, used his contacts from his days as an SIU Quality Control Manager for a major insurance company to land three major Property & Casualty insurance companies as clients. They made up exactly 3/4th of his work. The other 1/4th was comprised of a smattering of smaller Self-Insureds and (TPA) Third Party Administrators and local claims attorneys.

John was flying high and didn't know about the danger on the other side of the white puffy clouds he was about to enter.

REASONS WHY SALES GO FLAT

Service

This is the number one reason why customers switch providers. The customers have deadlines by which they need to make decisions. They have to make repeated contacts with the PI to chase down the reports. When they finally get ahold of the PI, the litany of excuses solidifies their decision to look elsewhere. They feel like they are talking to a kitchen remodeler!

If you cannot complete the majority of the assignment in the agreed upon time frame, let the client know as soon as possible what the problem is and how you are going to fix it. Keeping the client in the dark is the worst practice possible.

Process

You don't have one! Okay, I am not asking you to make McDonald's burgers and fries, but you must have a procedure for taking cases in, acknowledging assignments, and agreeing on the price and due dates. If you need to have a checklist in your assignment log to reinforce this, then do so, until you have committed these practices to memory. Do you jacket a paper file? Where do you keep the "stuff" that you have to forward to the client, such as police reports, DVDs, or sketches/drawings? This leads to the next category.

Product

An excellent report with average results will resonate better with the client than a poor report with great results. Before I produced reports for paying clients, I was the paying client. Some providers sent me the prettiest three-hole punch tabbed reports on professional letterhead, along with the hefty bill. As I sifted through the meticulously-formatted and perfectly-spelled words, with photos inserted by the latest word processing software, I had trouble finding the facts I needed to support a claim's payment or denial decision. As they say in Texas about talkers, not doers, such reports were "All Hat, No Cattle."

I had other providers that did an excellent investigation, but couldn't put two coherent sentences on paper. Getting them to send me a report **and a bill to pay** was like pulling teeth.

Today it is so much simpler. Build the templates for the reports that you regularly do and change out the information as needed. I tend to include my summary first then follow with the chronology of events and supporting documentation. I cover sheet the report with an invoice on letterhead.

Pricing

In my experience, flat rates work better than an acknowledged budget and much better than itemized bills.

Ask your client how often they prefer to be billed. A whopping bill at the end of a long-term assignment may get some pushback. If you charge by the hour and for mileage, the report should justify the time spent and where you went.

The client might pay you for your first case with them but will never call you again if they felt that you charged too much for the results they received. More often than not, this is because you didn't prepare them for the bill by **not** keeping them updated about the time and expense it took you to do your investigation. You failed to sell them on why the bill you sent them is appropriate. They were shocked when they received it.

Surprisingly, most private investigators **underprice** their services. I address that in more detail in the next book in this series. *How To Boost Your Private Investigations Business into Orbit.* The issue is not market-related. It is how you communicate your pricing on the front end and during the life of the case, so they don't have a heart attack when they get your bill.

So, if you have strengthened your **service, process, product**, and **pricing** then why are sales flat?

What is your brand? Are you attracting the right customers?

If you are the logical choice for your services, why isn't your inbox full of assignments or your phone ringing constantly from potential customers?

It boils down to lead generation, qualifying prospects, getting the assignment (converting), agreeing on price, fulfillment, testimonials, and referrals.

The checklist below will help you flesh out your one-page Marketing plan. That's the one on the wall in your workspace you look at every day, not the pretty one tucked away in your broken desk drawer you now have to fix over the weekend.

SECTION ONE: THE HONEYMOON IS OVER

CHECKLIST

Take 18 minutes to watch Simon Sinek's 18-minute TEDx talk on YouTube if you haven't already. He replaces Mission, Vision, and Value Statements with a Golden Circle of Why, How, and What. It is a much better way to align your passion with your customer's needs.

Why

What is your Why? What gets you up and working on a rainy Saturday?

How

How do you plan to go about getting to your Why?

What

What do you do for your customers to meet your Why?

Target Audience

Take the time to visualize who that person is or who that group is. The more detailed you make them, the better you will come to understand them, where to find them, and how to engage them.

Pricing

Can you make money turning a repetitive task like surveillance into an attractive flat rate? When you talk with the client, can you steer the conversation to a budget for spelled-out work to be performed by X date? If you must discuss an hourly rate, it only comes after you have thoroughly understood the client's needs. You then charge either a premium (and spell out why) or a discount from your premium rate (which is your standard rate), for which the customer is grateful.

Services

Don't try to be everything to everybody, unless you are the only game in town. The quicker and more efficient you are providing the services you can nail, the better. I will talk about nails in more detail later. For now, do what you do best. Your customers will begin telling you their other needs. There will be time to learn new skill sets, but for now, "stick to the knitting," as they say.

S.M.A.R.T. GOALS

Specific

I will do A, B and C.

For example, I will market the list of Trust, Probate, and Estate attorneys in my county and the adjacent county where I want to seek clients. I will do this on an ongoing basis. On Friday afternoons, I will contact each client where we had successful outcomes upon receipt of payment and ask for referrals.

Measurable

Following my call scripts, I will make 5 calls a day starting at 8:30 am Monday through Thursday, and I will enter my leads into the CRM.

Achievable

I will work with the Chair of the TP&E Bar association section to develop a lunch seminar on investigative topics relevant to their practices for presentation in May-June.

I will create a quarterly newsletter for my clients and prospect lists, highlighting successful cases that showcase my skill sets.

Relevant-Results

From my calls, I am looking to have callbacks from 65% of the leads. From those callbacks, I am looking to qualify and secure meetings with half of them. Half of the prospects will convert with assignments in the first six months.

Timely

I will hand-write and hand-deliver, where feasible, Thanksgiving cards to my best clients for this year.

Competition

Don't compete on price. It is a race to the bottom. Figure out what they do and offer something different or better, or something differently better. Learn from their mistakes. We will learn more about what they should be doing but aren't. Lucky you.

I don't spend much time thinking about competition these days. They are in the same boat as I am. You should be looking at the horizon for the storm clouds of well-funded start-ups that can disrupt your industry.

"What gets measured, gets done."

—Peter Drucker Management Guru

SECTION TWO: KEEPING SCORE

WHAT GETS MEASURED, GETS DONE

You track the hours you bill for each case, but do you track the hours you bill each day? Each month?

You receive inquiries (inbound marketing), but do you track them? What percentage convert to customers?

When you make calls to lists or pick up leads at seminars, lead groups or chamber of commerce sessions (outbound marketing), do you count them and segregate them into categories. Do you analyze what works and what doesn't?

Drucker said it best. "What gets measured, gets done." It's almost magical.

You will pay attention to the numbers you track. If you don't do any marketing that day, that week, that month, the ZEROES will stare back at you with an indignant look.

Conversely, when you see the number of calls you make (dialing for dollars) and the number of connections you make which result in appointments granted and assignments generated, you feel a sense of accomplishment. You see yourself putting a plan into action and how well it's working.

It becomes very plain to see you are engaged in a plan. Can you improve your message? Do you need to change your scripts? Are you talking too much during the presentations? Are you teasing out the client's real objections? Do your solutions meet their needs?

The investigator—oops, I meant to say the seller of investigative solutions—leaves a presentation meeting wondering why they didn't close the sale and thinks about what they need to change or improve. How much different is that from doing a cold call interview on a rainy night in a lousy neighborhood? Did you come at the right time for the witness? In the first fifteen seconds, while they sized you up, did you frame the issue and establish rapport? Did you have visuals to thrust in the door before they closed it on you? Did you have your rescue question ready to revive a stalled conversation?

Why do I juxtapose a street interview with a reduced sales call?

You weren't a great interviewer when you started, but you saw other investigative mentors, and you learned. It is the same with a sales call. You have to learn something new, and maybe a little foreign to your nature, and it's difficult. You are doing it without a mentor in most cases. I can say from experience, plan the work and work the plan. You might get tongue-tied the first couple of dials/callbacks or meetings/discussions, but with time, you'll relax, and it becomes fun. Yes, fun!

Time Management

I cannot stress this enough. Track your time. Are you nimble with your smartphone? Enter the time spent on tasks in your favorite app. When the ice age ended, and I came out of my cave, I used a pocket Day-timer. I tracked time by the quarter hour every day for years. It was automatic. It served as my record for billable time on cases, but I also tracked non-billable, travel, administrative, managerial, and supervisory time. Owner duties and bookkeeping were added when I went out on my own. Day in and day out, rain or shine, whether I felt like it or not. 52 to 56 hours a week were commonly tracked. Sometimes it jumped up to 60 and 70 hours, but only when I was cranking out more work or planning a new campaign.

It must have been around 1990 or 1991, years before my 1997 launch of Independent Special Investigations, that I learned the name of what the nuns called my lack of "self-control" or "obedience," those behavior labels on the left side of my report card. My scatter-brained hectic lifestyle was given the label ADD, Attention Deficit Disorder. Finally, I got an answer to why I was the way I was.

Saying good-bye to the good Sisters of Mercy, after thirteen years of Catholic schooling, I was ill-prepared for the rigors and freedom of college. With bad grades and a low draft number, I learned if I didn't get my act together, my next stop would be the University of South Vietnam, Mekong Delta campus, School of Warfare. I came back my sophomore year with a determination to succeed and to graduate. I was able to schedule afternoon classes, as I slept all morning because I started studying after 10 pm when the dorms quieted down. Nicotine, caffeine, and noise-canceling headphones quelled the distractions. I read and highlighted the text books and wrote notes furiously in class. I re-read the highlights and notes on Friday nights. I found study buddies for the classes that were Greek to me.

At home on Thanksgiving break, my mom was stunned to find out I was actually studying at the local community college library when she brought me a lunch one day. The amount of effort didn't immediately transfer into higher grades, but I didn't have to worry about exchanging my Criminology textbooks for an M-16.

Junior year, I made the dean's list, and in my senior year, I received back-to-back 4.0s.

I am not bragging here, just talking about turning a weakness into a strength. It was hard. There were no short cuts. I had to fall a lot before I could walk but, with time, it got easier.

Managing your time and working your plan is the key to marketing. Setting aside time for the to-do list where you are clear on your goals is paramount, but mostly measure your progress.

Drucker was not a dummy.

Critical Items First Thing In The Morning

Get your desk ready for marketing. The reports to bill out, non-sales emails to return, and the bookkeeping can wait. Other than confirming your appointments for the day, focus on your marketing.

I will tell you this secret: the sirens of email and Facebook will call you; ignore them. Putting the finishing touches on the report to bill out is very tempting, but it can be done later when your energy is lower. You have some easy stuff on your to-do list to check off. Wait, there will be time later. Fight the distractions and get to work on the life's blood of your business, sales, and marketing.

For those folks who rely on their website to generate inbound leads, it is like going out to the garden in the morning while the dew is still on the vine. Listen to the calls that came into the dedicated answer line. Return them right away. Emails to the contact form? Give a personalized reply and ask them to engage you by phone, if they can, for a free consultation. Qualify and convert. Sell and up-sell, if their situation warrants it. Start filling the pipeline. Each day that passes, the prospect may go to a lower-cost provider who will pick up the phone on the first ring. Each day that passes, their interest may wane.

For outbound marketing, called that because you are reaching **out**, there is a process to follow in identifying your leads, calling or emailing leads, calling leads or emailing again to leave a slightly different message, and talking to the leads with the singular goal of qualifying the prospect and getting the appointment. Can you meet in person? Great. If not, can you give them a link to an app where they can see you and your presentation materials? I suggest Skype or Screenflow, Google Drive Presentation with Keynote, or PowerPoint.

Resist the urge to send them your stuff by email or snail mail. You can't possibly know how to meet their needs without knowing what their pain or fear is.

People will buy from you when they know, like, and trust you. Separate yourself from the herd by providing a listening platform for your prospect's needs. More listening and less talking allow you to seize the opportunity to ask for the 15 minutes you need to move them from not interested in interested in meeting you.

On the days you have a marketing appointment, work your investigative assignments around that marketing call.

What about prospects that you cannot drive to? Is it cost-effective to fly to meet a customer? I would say yes if you can make up the cost of the airport parking, flight, hotel, meals, and time away from billing with the case, or in the first 5-6 cases with the potential of more. Pre-qualifying these leads are paramount.

Do this heavy-lifting first thing in the morning. Plan your first investigative appointments to allow you to market and drive to your first stop.

> You will find if you get in the habit of doing your marketing first thing, it gets done.

CRM For B2C, B2C, P2P

Part of keeping score is how you retain your marketing leads.

- ACT in the Windows platform
- Insightly CRM in Apple
- Hubspot
- Zapier if you are looking to integrate your CRM with other applications
- Salesforce is the big daddy of them all

They all give you features and benefits that range in cost from a couple of hundred dollars a year to a couple thousand. Smaller platforms might mean you may have to keystroke the same data into your assignment log, accounting software, and email lists. Zapier might ease that pain, as it helps integrate popular applications.

The most important feature is the follow-up feature. You meet a prospect at a gathering, or you make a call and leave a message. In your CRM you note whom you talked with, the date, and a note, then s**chedule a date and time for the follow-up**. Some mornings, I sit down at my desk and have an hour's worth of follow-up calls to make. They are all queued up.

What if you were able to import hundreds or thousands of qualified leads into your CRM? What if you were able to send them then a six-email autoresponder sequence with links to your website and your sales funnel?

What would a four percent conversion rate on a thousand leads with a profit margin of 50% on an average sale of $800.00 for a Flat Rate look like in your bank account? Hint: $16,000.

Would you pay $1.00 a lead or $1,000 for that list? With a 16:1 rate of return, you would do that every time.

However, wait, there's more. With a better marketing message, could you increase your conversions to say 6%? Maybe add an up-sell at the end of the sale to increase the profit margin to 60% on a higher $999 sale for your flat rate and premium background check (you could go with $1,000 for the sake of round numbers, but there's a bit of marketing psychology to that $999).

Now that original $1.00 per lead cost brings in $36,000 just on 2% more in conversions with 10% more on margin on $200 more on the average sale. Get the picture?

This works exceptionally well in the B2C world where the customer is a one-time buyer, but what if you could cross-sell the B2C customer with another service, or have an affiliate link with other professionals that could service that customer with follow-up services? Divorce attorneys or CPAs come to mind.

None of this, so far, includes the referral commission program your customers could enter. With a profit margin on your higher end offerings of 60%, you could easily give your customers 10% for each referral that results in a case, plus a 10% discount given to the referred customer.

Keep an email list of your customers. You might be surprised how sending them a follow-up email 60-90 days after the one-time service, thanking them for the assignment and mentioning the referral program in a non-salesy or spammy way, could result in follow-up work for them on top of what you have already done. Gee, all you did was thank them.

Add in testimonials, and you get the picture.

All this talk of CRM and email lists might make your head swim but look at it this way: today's prospect may become next year's customer. If you rely on them to dig your business card out of their desk drawer or go searching for your email, you have less chance of connecting with them than if you sent them an occasional news release, free report, newsletter or sales promotion.

For instance, at the time of this writing, I am running a "Summer Special" offering 10% off all my flat rates for first-time customers. That sale has an "act now" feel as I end it on Labor Day. With 10 days to go, I have landed 9 new customers and $5,400 from an email blast to 239 prospects that took me 45 minutes to compose in MailChimp's Constant Contact.

Personally, I use Insightly CRM in conjunction with MailChimp and two Numbers (Excel) spreadsheets, for prospects and customers respectively. I use customer billing templates in Pages for my reports and invoices and have my QuickBooks preloaded with the customer data. I also keystroke out a seven-field assignment log.

For a B2C focus, your website buildout should have, at a bare minimum, a contact form and email solution to capture leads. You may have to move them manually into a CRM if you don't use an integration app like Zapier.

With B2B, it is imperative to capture and enter Prospect data into a CRM where you track a prospect's progress through your sales funnel.

We will talk about P2P with Tony's sample below.

Saturday Morning Marketing Projects

Plan them and execute them. It is so easy to slough off any of your repetitive tasks to Saturday morning or Sunday, depending on your weekend commitments, but if you carve out time to work on the occasional project, say from 8 am to 10 am, you can boost your marketing exponentially without giving up half your weekend.

Some ideas of Saturday morning marketing projects are:

- Work on creating or updating your Free Report
- Compose a mail campaign for your Newsletter

- Work on creating or updating your Free Checklist
- The Testimonial Ask
- Promotions
- Sales Special
- News Release
- Tweak the website with new content
- Add new video or written testimonials
- Develop or update your brochures or sales sheets (AKA leave-behinds or collateral)

Put these projects on the calendar as the opportunities arise. As a content provider, you want to offer value to your prospects and clients. Make it easier for the former to know, like, and trust you and give the latter more reason to stay with you and not succumb to the temptations of your competitors, who are knocking on their doors constantly.

I did use the words 'content provider' on purpose. You self-identify as an investigator first, and it is not always intuitive to think about yourself as a content provider. Think of it this way, before someone will part with their own or their company's money, they would like to know more about the investigator who might be able to meet their needs. The more your content creates a likable bond with the lead, the more they will see themselves prospectively trusting you with the most serious problem they are facing or have to get off their desk. If your content identifies their fears and provides a reasonable solution to their problem, the less resistance they will have to select you for their private investigation needs.

Old-Fashioned Flip Chart

A simple flip chart sits behind me in my office. The top sheet, right now, is all about the Third Quarter. Across the top are nine categories that I measure. Along the side is the week, ending on Saturday.

Thirteen weeks a quarter, four quarters a year. The first two quarters are taped on the wall above my side table. With a glance, I can see how I am doing. Last year's numbers are kept handy. I can pull out the Third Quarter from last year for easy side-by-side comparison and see that I'm doing better this quarter than the same time last year.

This is what I measure:

- Weekly Billing goal: example $4,270
- Weekly "Actuals": example $4,690
- Delta Example: "$420" or "-$420"
- Color-coded by specialty area:
- Stick count of Flat rates
- Stick count of Budget cases
- Stick count of Hourly cases
- Stick count of leads called
- Stick count of callbacks
- Stick count of appointments made

The numbers don't lie. Am I making goal? Are my marketing efforts generating the cases I want to work? Am I doing the marketing I said I would do? Am I getting appointments?

Okay, it's summertime, but that doesn't mean I don't market. Yes, my clients take vacations in the summer, but they don't take the whole summer off. No excuses.

That flip chart keeps me honest and shows me the most important numbers for my business. Mr. Drucker would be proud of me and my very simple tracking device.

How many leads became how many prospects, turned into how

many appointments, resulted in how many cases? What kind of cases paid me how much money? If I keep putting the numbers on the flip chart and keep it where I can't hide from it, I am motivated to maintain my numbers in the black column and to keep the numbers out of the red column.

The best marketing plan, with the best tools and the most compelling message aligned with your target audience's needs, won't be worth a hill of beans if you don't prioritize the time actually to do the marketing.

I turned time management and organization challenges from a weakness into a strength, and I want to share my learnings at the School of Hard Knocks with you.

I guess you can blame it on my ADD.

You are welcome.

"Your Brand is what other people say about you."

—Jeff Bezos, CEO founder Amazon

SECTION THREE: BRANDING

WHAT DOES YOUR WEBSITE REALLY SAY?

I am in Western New York as I type this. I type "Private Investigator" into the search bar in my browser. The first four searches are paid ads for Online PI firms that specialize in Fidelity Investigations. Most of those firms will take your money and send out to a local PI for cents on the dollar. You will deal with a firm that is pandering to the masses.

I click on one of the first PIs who comes up after the paid ads, in the organic search results. Their Home page loads showing royalty-free stock photos of busy streets and skylines. Pretty generic stuff. Nothing compelling. The contact form pop-up loads before the rest of the Home Page and you have to dismiss it to read the Home Page content when it finally loads. I repeat, I had to X out of the contact form and close it to read the home page. Will I bother to search out the contact form after I closed it?

The portrait of the owner shows up in a thumbnail. A thumbnail! I've seen better mugshots, quite frankly. It is not a professionally taken photograph—if it was, the PI should get their money back. A run-on block of text goes on and on about the lineage of the company and how they come from a family of former Law

Enforcement. I tell you there is **nothing** on that first page that addresses the customer or their wants, needs, or fears. Nada. To me, the home page screams, "We are more important than you are!"

Next, you scroll down to a mis-mash of services. B2B, B2C, Security Guard Service, Very Specialized Debugging.

When everybody is your target audience, you are connecting with nobody.

The site offers no testimonials and no pictures of satisfied persons or companies.

So, I move on to the next site in my search results. I see one tag line about the customer's needs, then a confusing Nav bar of services and directions. This PI is a Surveillance hammer in search of Surveillance nails.

Are they B2B or B2C? Today it is a case about a cheating spouse. Tomorrow it is a case about a disabled man out on Workers Comp helping a buddy move. Who is the target audience? They don't say.

Then there is a video. It is a disjointed, re-purposed video that talks about the PI coming from the long line of cops, the gratuitous shot of guns and very little about the client's needs. I didn't watch it all the way through.

Remember, a video of satisfied customer talks to the customer. This site's video talked to the ego of the PI, in my humble opinion. Next.

The next website is slick. It has a slider of stock photos of CIA types flashing across the top third. They are generalists pretending to be specialists. We do everything for everybody, but we do it well. They have a chatbot. I didn't bother. I scanned the site to see if they had any testimonials or copy that speaks to the needs, wants or fears of at least one type of client. They can't provide that because they are trying to be everything to everybody.

However, because they have a slick website, they can charge a premium. Is there anything there that marries a benefit or feature to a need or a want? Nope. Nada. Nyet.

I have to stop. You get the picture. Now go and type in "Private Investigator" and your bustling burg's name into your browser search bar and see what turns up for you.

Do the websites have cutesy names or do they say what they do individually? Bonus points for a website with a specific customer need baked in. The first website I built was www.siuonline.com. My company name in the B2B sphere was Independent Special Investigations, LLC. My target audience was SIU managers and Claims adjusters. I couldn't make it any clearer.

Do the names of the firms have a name that plays to the Gunslinging Gumshoe or Shameless Seamus stereotype? Deduct points for pictures of owners depicting people for whom, if they were standing on her front porch, you would tell your mother not to open the door.

Are the sites customer-focused? Do they spend more time on their own needs and wants to move money from a yet-to-be-described customer, than the needs and wants of the customer?

Do they throw up on you in their About Page? Is there any connection between their background and the specific needs of their target audience?

Do they offer a press release, newsletter, checklist, free report, eBook, or video testimonial?

Your brand is what your customer says about you. What do their customers say about them? Is the target market identified? How are objections and resistance dealt with right on the home page?

SECTION THREE: BRANDING

Is there any Gun-slinging Gumshoe or Shameless Seamus stuff there?

Let's say you are a Personal Injury or Family Law attorney looking to replace your present investigative solution and you have one of these firms referred to you from another lawyer that you trust. You compare this website with the paid ads or other top of the page search returns in Connecticut and tell me, what would you do?

In the P2P market, your target market already has a solution. I learned I have to keep my face out there for that time when that other PI moves to Florida, becomes too old, tired, or sick to work, or for those PIs who decide to quit without telling their customers. After a couple of unreturned phone messages, the client gets the picture.

The professional in need of an investigator will reach out to their friends in the business, whom they **know, like, and trust** to ask for a referral to a PI that their friend, you guessed it, knows, likes, and trusts.

Now, let's talk about your website:

Can you, or someone you can talk to 24/7, add, subtract, or modify content easily?

Does your website take forever to load?

Is it Search Engine Optimized for keywords your customers will use in their searches?

Access your website from your smartphone or tablet. More people search from their phones these days. What does your website look like on the phone?

Does your company name and logo (including colors and fonts) speak to your target audience?

Does your content address the wants and needs of your target audience?

Do you have a target audience?

Who is your ideal customer?

What do they eat for breakfast? Okay, that's going a little too far, but remember if "everybody" your target audience then you are talking to nobody. Get serious about exactly who you want to talk to and understand their habits.

Do your benefits and features give you a unique edge over the competition?

How can you phrase it to express that you are better, faster, and less expensive than the herd? (Getting the job done right the first time is less expensive, charging a flat rate where you have a healthy profit margin is less expensive than the unknown in the client's mind.)

Being the cheapest has you in first place in the race to the bottom. You provide a professional service, not a commodity. More on that later.

Do your images express what you are trying to say to your target audience? Do they detract from your message? If you have no photos or graphics, why not?

Can the client read a News Release? Can they click on a Newspaper headline, or see a video of a TV report? This is social proof of how good you are.

Do you give the target audience a checklist, free report, eBook, or other value that keeps them thinking about you and what you can do for them?

What about your testimonials? It doesn't matter if you are B2C, B2B, P2P, or hybrid. Testimonials pre-qualify your prospect. If

SECTION THREE: BRANDING

the viewer can stand in the shoes of the person giving a testimonial, they are on the road to knowing, liking, and trusting you.

What is your CTA? That is your Call To Action. "Act Now!" "Don't Delay!" "Call or text me at (123) 456-7890 to discuss your needs. I will pick up my phone or call you right back when I get out of the shower."

Does each page have a CTA at the bottom with your phone or email? In today's connected world, "operators are standing by," because the prospect's connection to you is from their smartphone to yours. Live Chat in the B2C world is a CTA. In the business or professional world, the prospect is more apt to call or email you directly.

WHAT DOES YOUR COLLATERAL REALLY SAY?

What is collateral? Answer: business cards, brochures, flyers, leave-behinds, and promotional sheets. Digitally speaking, it could be your newsletters and free reports, or price schedules (although, people smarter than me say not to have your hourly rate on your website—flat rates or promotional rates are different).

Jimmie Mesis, the former owner of PI Magazine, has an answer for that question about rates. He always responds with, "It depends." He recommends you ask questions about the assignment to qualify the prospect, learn what has already been done, the urgency, and what they have budgeted for the work. I will tell you more about Jimmie and how you and he can make money together in *How to Boost your PI Business into Orbit*.

Dr. Jeffrey Lant, in his seminal work *Cash Copy* back in 1989, wrote that most marketing copy:

Doesn't target people who need you

Doesn't speak directly to these people

Doesn't tell these people precisely what you can do for them

Doesn't work to allay their anxieties about taking immediate action

Doesn't use past buyer testimonials indicating specific results attuned to get prospects to buy

Doesn't hammer home a consistent believable, client-centered message.

He advises, "The best marketing copy is an exciting dialogue between two people—you, the seller, and the single prospect/buyer who is reading what you have to say about them, their problem, and how you will solve it."

John says:

Identify their needs and how they will benefit from your service. Lead with needs, follow with benefits.

What are their fears, how can your services address their fears?

Create your target customer and talk to them.

Every marketing piece has to have a Call To Action.

Can you offer a time-sensitive discount, free consultation, or free report (in exchange for their email)?

Separate your company from the herd. My company competes with a lot of retired coppers. In face-to-face meetings, I say that I am **not** retired. I am not tired, and the best is yet to come.

Tease out your Unique Selling Proposition (USP).

Back in 1997-1998, I wrote this about my first company:

INDEPENDENT SPECIAL INVESTIGATIONS

Was formed to bridge the widening gap between Independent Adjusters and Private Investigators.

Independent adjusters know policy coverage and claims-handling procedures and specialize in the adjustment of the claim.

Private investigators know how to investigate but lack the claims knowledge to service the Property and Casualty Insurance Industry amongst a diverse clientele.

No one combines claims experience with ins. fraud investigation expertise until now

SECTION THREE: BRANDING

TESTIMONIALS

Here is a sample email to your satisfied client who just paid you and sent a thank you note with their check.

Hi Ed or Edna:

Thank you so much for your kind words. I am glad the case turned out well for you. Could I ask you to please give me a testimonial?

I have made it easy for you to provide me with one—it should only take a moment. As I recall, you told me you had a trial date looming and needed to contact a witness who you just learned about. All your attempts to locate that witness had failed. I answered the phone on the second ring, and we talked about your needs. By talking about your case, I teased out that other persons whom the witness worked with were identified. In quick order, I located one of the workers and they told me the witness's ex-wife's name. I was able to find her, and she told me that her ex was on probation in the adjoining county. I made contact with the witness at his next probation appointment and served him with a subpoena to appear. If you agree, I can write something up for you.

SECTION THREE: BRANDING

Just to be sure, may I use your last name and title in the testimonial?

I will send it to you for your review and approval.

Thanks again

Jack or Jackie, Owner

Brass City Investigations

A day later……

Hi Ed or Edna

Here is the testimonial. I hope you like it:

I had a trial date in 12 days and just learned about a witness whom I could not find. I got hold of Jack or Jackie at Brass City Investigations right away, and they combined their computer and people skills to not only find the guy living in Springfield but also to serve him in time. His testimony made all the difference at trial, and my client was ecstatic. The work was professional, performed quickly and the bill was exactly what they quoted.

-Ed or Edna Jablocknicki, Attorney at Law

If you agree, I will use this in my brochures and on my website.

Thanks

Jack or Jackie, Owner

Brass City Investigations

If for some arcane reason you are put off by supplying the client with a well-crafted testimonial that they agree to, you may instead give them a template.

Hi Ed or Edna:

Thank you for your kind words. I am glad the case worked out well for you. Could I impose on you for a minute to provide me with a testimonial that I can use on my website and in the brochure I am working on?

Could you describe the problem you had and how easy it was for us to talk? My clients have that problem often.

Can you add how easy it was for us to brainstorm the solution? This will help the reader want to trust me with their problem too.

In your own words, could you then describe what we did for you and how that helped your situation become very clear?

How did that make you or your client feel?

A quick ending on how fast we did the work and our pricing with your full business signature would be perfect.

Whaddya think? Can you help us find more great clients like you?

Sincerely Jack or Jackie, Owner

Brass City Investigations

SUMMARY

All of this leads to permitting you to rebrand and to refresh your website and your collateral. I can feel your "sunk-cost bias" pressing down on you. I can hear you say, "I spent X number of dollars or number of hours just building my site. Am I just going to throw out those beautiful brochures I just had printed up?"

Just remember the words of Jeff Bezos. **Branding is what other people say you are.** His little company Amazon is trading today for a share price where I wish a had a few hundred shares —just saying

SUMMARY

"When you hunt wildebeest, you go to their watering hole."

—John A. Hoda, CLI, CFE

SECTION FOUR: TARGETING THE RIGHT AUDIENCE

WHERE DOES YOUR TARGET AUDIENCE DRINK?

Stay with me on this. There is a good story coming.

One PI firm I know sponsors a co-ed softball team in an affluent town. Twenty-Somethings and Thirty-Somethings are playing softball after work. Each team plays the PI's team at least twice a summer. The PI's players are wearing their company name and logo on their IBM blue jerseys. Most of these players are the PI's young employees, and the PI pays their tab to go to the local watering hole where the teams congregate.

A couple of hundred age-appropriate people (infidelity investigation prospects) meet the PI's people in a relaxed setting. Alcohol and pub grub make for relaxed conversations. Those couple of hundred people have thousands of relatives. Is it possible that maybe more than a handful may not be in good relationships? Those softball players usually play for the company they work for. How many co-workers do they have? Those players have hair stylists, gym buddies, play date parents, dog park attendees. You get the picture.

Do the professionals you market have annual, quarterly, or monthly meetings? Can you be a speaker? Can you put together a

SECTION FOUR: TARGETING THE RIGHT AUDIENCE

"Seven Deadly Sins" PowerPoint that places your services directly in the path of their needs? Can you sponsor the cocktail hour?

How about a vendor table with a table skirt embroidered with your company name and logo on it? You could easily carry in a couple stand-up displays with content matching your services to that wildebeest's need.

Tip: Keep your audience in mind. Don't bring your signage and leave-behinds for lions and tigers to the wildebeest watering hole.

Everybody loves to hear war stories from Private Investigators. Can you offer to speak at the Chamber of Commerce, the Kiwanis, or The Rotary Club? The same multiplier is in effect as the softball league, except you are trading the jerseys and ball caps for nicely-tailored power suits.

Holiday cheer and holiday parties. Golf outings. Association Year-end parties or mid-summer picnics. Go to where your prospects gather.

Can you drop off reports in person to your client and ask them for referrals within the building or nearby?

It works like this:

"Hi Chris, I was just dropping off a report of a (briefly describe the successful investigation) with Pat Client on the eighth floor, and Pat told me to come by and introduce myself. Pat told me you have a similar practice. I'm curious. How do you meet your investigative needs?"

Out of politeness to their colleague, Pat, they will spend a minute with you, and you can qualify this prospect.

If they are a good fit, say to them, "I know you're busy now, but can I come back next Thursday before court and explore your needs for 15 minutes. How does that sound?"

Hint: Next Thursday before court usually works and if it doesn't, you have them giving you an alternate time and date. It's incredible to see how simple this is.

"Smokestacking" refers to an old-fashion route salesperson coming into a new town. They would look for the smokestacks and make a cold call, or they would walk the length of Main Street and stop in each store, say hello, leave a card and ask the shopkeeper if they could tell the salesperson whom they should talk to.

In today's world, when you are working a case on the street, and you literally have to walk by a prospect's office to get to your car. Do you make a quick detour?

Do you keep business cards, press releases, brochures, and price sheets in your folio?

Which brings me to the question of how you attire yourself when you are on the street. I always dress for the most important person I have to establish rapport with that day. I dress differently for cold call door knocks in a not-so-nice neighborhood than I do for an appointment with a prospect. I would instead tell my prospect the story of why I am wearing a polo and khakis than explain to a witness why the older man that I am is wearing a business suit and knocking on their door. I think the former would be more understanding than the latter. What do you think?

For years, my favorite attorney has invited me to his holiday party. It is The Event to go to every year. This large law firm invites their own families and tons of other attorneys-spouses as well. They rent a five-star hotel ballroom and have a locally renowned jazz band play.

Attendees eat their way around the room with the best hand-carved meats, hand-rolled sushi, and hand-made desserts. I'll stop there. You get the picture, and it's making me hungry.

Anyway, most of those previous years, my favorite attorney sat on a local town board, and they met on the same weeknight as the party, but in 2012, the dates didn't match up, and he attended his own company's holiday party.

I arrived early and was chatting him up about a case I had just done for him.

It was mid-December, and I had taken a sandwich board to a busy intersection on the same day of the week, at the same time during morning rush hour as the accident. The sandwich board read, "Did you see the motorcycle and bicycle accident in October? Call John Hoda at (123)-456-7890"

A polar vortex had our little town in an Arctic grip of sub-zero weather that day. It was freezing cold, just after dawn, and my attorney was very appreciative.

What made this case special and worth re-telling is the motorcycle was being operated by a police officer who had just finished working the midnight shift and was gunning it to beat the light. The boy on the bicycle was entering the far side of the intersection on a green light before the collision. When the motorcycle hit him, he flew high in the air. His left leg required multiple surgeries, and the possibility of walking was still up in the air.

Can you imagine what the police report said? Were there any witnesses noted? What do you think? This is why I had to find a creative solution. More importantly, what do you think the witnesses I was searching for would say?

It was this story of the sandwich board that my favorite attorney told his friends as they walked into the party. These were other high-powered attorneys who respected him and trusted him. I would go fetch drinks and appetizers for my favorite attorney between times he regaled his steady stream friends with this story of my creativity.

I haven't missed any of their parties since that night.

General versus Specific

Does your website call to the whole jungle or one or two related species?

Are you hunting with a sawed-off shotgun or with a hunting rifle?

Can you meet the needs of the general public with several services? Absolutely.

Looking at the reverse, should you be offering those services to the general consumer B2C and B2B simultaneously? I argue not. If you are hunting B2C and a B2B wanders in, you can take your shot, but don't start watering down your marketing message. Be specific in your message to exactly who you want to talk to. Talking to everybody means you are addressing nobody. Be specific.

User versus Buyer

This is an easier decision in most cases. You talk to the person with fears, needs, and a desire for change with their issue. Once you have the investigative objective and can determine the cost, you make a presentation to the buyer with high, medium, and low pricing (unless the assignment can be done quickly with a flat rate, then you pitch that). A two-step sales pitch is required with the user and the ultimate buyer. Never forget who writes the check. That can become a nasty surprise.

What about in B2B where you want to become a service provider for many users of the business you are targeting such as a Claims Department, Corporations, Governmental agencies, Chain Retailers, or Franchisors. Do you create a suite of services to meet the needs of an entire industry? Whom do you pitch and what is your pitch? How is your pitch to a Claims VP different than to an SIU manager? I will address that question in Section Eight-Flying Fortress.

SECTION FOUR: TARGETING THE RIGHT AUDIENCE

Going Wide versus Going Deep

There are arguments on both sides for this. The deeper you go, the more specialized your services are and the more you can charge. In a lifestyle business, having a specialty for a loyal group of high-paying clients is ideal. On the other hand, market forces out of your control may cause that business to dry up. Having a broader customer base smooths out the sales cycles. In both cases, all your marketing materials and your message should be consistent with the audience.

Tony's detectives in Mid-town Manhattan handle many financial crimes and work with the Feds on joint cases regardless of who was the primary case investigator. Tony is well-positioned to approach the professionals in Queens about his services. Their needs become more evident to him as they talk about their civil remedies. Finding witnesses and interviewing them becomes his most-requested service, followed by asset checks of the targets. Tony learns to suggest the asset check immediately after he gets evidence on the target, so the client will know if it is worth going after the target with more costly litigation.

CPAs in his home borough work with hundreds of small businesses who are getting ripped off by employees, vendors, sub-contractors, and dead-beat customers. They turn to Tony to find the evidence and help them bring the cases to small business attorneys to prosecute the thefts and frauds civilly. Those attorneys begin using him on their other cases with larger clients. The Russo & Associates brand is starting to form with the triangle of CPAs, Small Business Attorneys, and mid-size corporations in Queens.

However, it is his friend, the former DA, that tells Tony he has an innocent client sitting out in Nassau County jail. Tony reviews the discovery into the murder case and goes about his investigation. He locates witnesses that completely discredit the sole eyewitness while bolstering the alibi witnesses the locals had ignored. The Nassau County DA has to drop the case. Tony is there when his attorney's client is released from jail. The front-page headline and photo of the trio accompany the article in which the attorney credits Tony for gathering the evidence of his client's innocence. Tony uploads the video of the TV reports and the Newspaper Headlines to his website.

Tony catches some gas from his former squad, but in the end, they know Tony is a straight-shooter and that he never let them get away with cutting corners or taking short-cuts like what happened in this case. Tony had never considered working Criminal Defense, but in the days following that headliner, he receives overtures from other Nassau County Criminal Defense Attorneys. He doesn't want to go against NYPD, his former employer of nearly three decades, but has no problem with taking on the boys and girls in blue in the adjoining county. This work energizes him. He had never considered it as a possibility, and now he looks forward to the cases he reviews for those Defense lawyers.

Truth Be Told Investigations, Inc. captures leads when prospects give their email to Beth to obtain a Free Report. She takes turns with her employee answering the Chat Live calls and can convert the calls into paying customers by walking them through the shopping cart. Her outbound marketing to the high-end hair salons, wellness centers nail salons, beauty shops, and gyms is focused on upscale women in Austin's booming economy. After six months of modest pricing, she increases her hourly and flat rates twice without any clients blinking an eye. The split is also showing her the upscale clients are coming from the outbound marketing almost exclusively. She and Mary can say bye-bye to the Armored Guard jobs when the cash flow forecasts show they are way ahead of schedule. Beth's professionalism and processes are appreciated by her customers which increases her word of mouth referrals. Her numbers are evenly split between inbound from her website and outbound from her marketing to upscale women where they congregate. However, outbound marketing is providing more than twice the income per assignment. She needs to double in size and knows her processes have to absorb the added administrative time. Her brand is slowly moving from taking all comers to meeting the needs of higher-paying longer-tail cases. The work is also bringing her in contact with Austin's high-end law firms, who are contacting her to conduct more detailed Open-source Intelligence (OSINT) investigations, which pay very well.

Independent Special Investigations grew on schedule and expanded into insurance surveillance. John's marketing stalled as he did everything except the bookkeeping. His training was hands-on, and his new employees accompanied him as he handled cases. Later, he accompanied them until they were comfortable with the work and managed their own caseload. The work took them from Connecticut into Long Island and NYC, as well as Boston and Providence. They drove longer distances, and the clients balked at paying for extensive travel time and mileage. John created billing points for the clients, but still paid his employees' drive time and mileage, portal to portal. The billing points cut into profit margins, and his next hires had to be in NYC and Massachusetts. Revenues were growing, but so were expenses. The second year of ISI showed mixed results. Still, John and his top employee created in-house training seminars for his customers and the annual IASIU in Dallas, Texas. He attended local state association lunch meetings in Connecticut, Massachusetts, and Rhode Island. He created a quarterly newsletter for his customers, and his sub-contracted secretary mailed them out for him.

John was one busy hombre. He brought his expertise to his target audience where they worked and where they congregated.

SECTION FOUR: TARGETING THE RIGHT AUDIENCE

SUMMARY

As you begin to learn who your best customers are, keep looking at your message and make sure you are talking to the people you want to reach. Marketing is not a spectator sport for Private Investigation businesses. You can see the prospects meet for work, then eat and drink for play. You have to manage your time to go to these events. Some may require late evenings while others may require you to travel to conferences. Your marketing is the lifeblood of your business, and you have to sacrifice billing time to invest.

SECTION FOUR: TARGETING THE RIGHT AUDIENCE

CHECKLIST

- Chamber of Commerce Leads groups
- BNI (Business Network International) groups
- Rotary, Kiwanis, Library nights
- Association meetings
- Conferences
- Bar association gatherings
- CPA association gatherings
- Golf outings
- Bowling or Softball leagues. (Sponsor a team if you're not a kegler or baller)
- Create a power point (i.e., Seven Deadly Sins) for your target audience Continuing Ed Requirements, or create their in-house training where their needs intersect with your services.
- Take the claim adjusters, paralegals, or CPAs' bookkeepers to lunch day.
- "Smokestack"—Do you keep marketing materials in your folio?
- Deliver brochures to other prospects in your client's building.

SECTION FOUR: TARGETING THE RIGHT AUDIENCE

"Makes sense to me, what do you think?"

—Stephan Schiffman from *Closing Techniques that Really Work*

SECTION FIVE:
GUESS WHAT? YOU ARE ALWAYS CLOSING.

BASICS OF SELLING

From *How To Launch Your Private Investigation Business: 90 Days To Lift Off*

John came to Independent Special Investigations with no sales skills and no marketing plan, per se. He had an old-fashioned Rolodex and long-standing relationships with many SIU managers who knew liked, and trusted him. He launched his company at a time when SIU units had hired as many investigators as the Claims Department budgets allowed, and the SIU managers needed to outsource investigations due to higher volume or geographic considerations. John exceeded their expectations and did so with reasonable pricing. He made believers with his work product and training presentations. He counted Insurance Companies Claims Departments and SIU units as his target audience and marketed at the local and regional level.

SECTION FIVE: GUESS WHAT? YOU ARE ALWAYS CLOSING

Tony is wondering all about this marketing and selling stuff. He thought he could do it, but now he is having second thoughts. After a short stint working in the trades as a laborer after high school, he decided to join the police department. What he feels about selling was gleaned from roles played Al Pacino in Glengarry Glen Ross and Leonardo DiCaprio in the Wolf of Wall Street. Not precisely good role models.

Selling has a bad connotation to him.

Then there is the barrage of telemarketing calls on his phone and pop-ups when he does a google search for the Mets score.

Worse, as he starts asking professionals how they market, he gets a blizzard of answers, and as a trained investigator, he realizes that they are as clueless as he is.

How do they stay in business? he wonders.

Tony realizes that this is a weakness and that his own pre-conceptions are getting in the way as well. He knows that he will make mistakes until he feels comfortable with listening to his clients' needs and learning how to meet them.

Beth is coming into this sales pipeline process with open eyes. She says very clearly, "My branding, marketing, and sales materials are all about the consumer. My services will allay their fears and help them with the decisions that they need to make."

She is building her business around her Why, How and What. She looks to other Service related e-Commerce sites and is honing her process to capture eye-balls and convert leads to prospects. This is the new language that she has to learn. Sitting in on prisoner of war debriefing sessions in Afghanistan taught her how to learn new languages and she has to learn the language of selling.

SECTION FIVE: GUESS WHAT? YOU ARE ALWAYS CLOSING

> Where you came from before deciding to market your Private Investigation business is as important as where will you go from here.

The mantra, "the marketing you do is better than the marketing you should do, but don't," combined with having a plan to market just 5 hours a week is a bridge to where you want to be.

This comes from a guy who openly said he would instead take out the trash than pick up the phone and market. What changed? Well, for one, the business climate. I will cover that in Section Eight: Flying Fortress.

Secondly, I learned one technique at a time and measured my progress. I studied what worked and more importantly, what didn't and why.

Slowly over time, I began to realize if I wanted to succeed as a Private Investigator in Business, I had to learn about business, and central to that premise was learning how to market and sell investigative services.

I had to make some hard decisions and decide what conferences and training seminars I would attend. Do I spend time and money on investigative classes or marketing classes?

I spoke about wanting to continually upgrade my investigative skills as my motivation.

Why do you resist sales and marketing activity? Does it leave a funny taste in your mouth? Are you disdainful of the process? Do you feel like a snake-oil salesperson?

I understand your feelings. Most professionals feel cheap when they have to hawk their wares, **the work should speak for itself, or so the thinking goes.**

Can you reframe those feelings?

Can you see that you offer a valuable service and people need it? Can you make more people aware that you can help them solve their problems?

I traveled the path from not knowing what I didn't know, to knowing what I didn't know.

Stated differently, I went from being unconsciously incompetent to becoming consciously incompetent. It was a difficult process, but I was determined to learn. Slowly, I began to know what steps to follow in what order.

With that came the confidence to grow my sales persona to where I could pitch a prospect on a return phone call, even as I was getting out of my car for a long walk to do a door knock. That didn't happen overnight. I had to take baby steps at first, and as my confidence grew, I began seeking out more courses on marketing.

A few years ago, I went to SumoCon in Austin, Texas, where I met Noah Kagan and the good folks at App Sumo. They are the Sumo wrestlers in the internet e-commerce arena. That's why I wanted Beth Clark to work there in the B2C world and have them chatting over tacos with her.

If your business model is B2C, you owe it to yourself to leverage your website with inbound marketing. Inbound means the prospects are looking for a solution to their problem and if you can give them value during their search phase and drip content to them with email autoresponders they can begin to know, like, and trust your business.

The following year, I traveled to Alexandria, Virginia, from Connecticut to immerse myself in the Ben Glass Law "Great Legal Marketing" course.

"Whoa, what's that?" you ask.

Why would I spend four days of time and all that money for tolls, two tanks of gas, three nights hotel, and food to learn marketing geared to lawyers?

My reasons were two-fold. Where else could I have a large group of my sample target audience under one roof for four days? They were under no sales pressure from me, and I was able to ask them what they valued in a Private Investigator and what would motivate them to switch service providers? The trip was worth the consensus of answers I received.

As a bonus, I watched how Family Law, Personal Injury, and Disability practitioners overcame their fears and prejudices and learned to begin employing strategies in their businesses. Just the "before and after" recordings of how some law firms answered their phones was the best comedic attention grabber of the conference.

Then there was the montage of TV spots where the lawyers looked tough, acted tough, and talked about themselves. Later, the client-focused TV spots were aired. A handful of converts allowed Ben to play their own TV spots before and after applying what they learned through the GLM course.

Combined with other client-focused strategies, graphs on the ballroom screens showed growth in the number of cases taken, per case average settlement/verdict growth, and eye-popping, chart-topping revenues. Ben also emphasized taking the stress out of their business by empowering others and honing processes so they could concentrate on what they did best.

Great lawyers were learning how to become good marketers.

I will tell you a secret. Lawyers are a risk-averse bunch and are loathe to change. However, these attendees had reached a pain point—they had been spinning their wheels or revving in low gear, not realizing the full potential of their practices for a long time.

Something had to change. They were ready to address their pain.

Let me save you some pain, time, and money. Just bring an open mind and plan to incorporate one or two ideas you learn here for five hours a week to start.

SECTION FIVE: GUESS WHAT? YOU ARE ALWAYS CLOSING

A.I.D.A.

Attention

The prospect is looking to address a pain point. They are going on the Internet to find a solution. Professionals tend to reach out to other professionals and ask for a referral. Separate yourself from the herd by talking directly to them in your marketing copy. Again, from Dr. Jeffrey Lant's 1989 *Cash Copy*, in two words, you care.

- Care to understand what your prospects are trying to accomplish.
- Care to let them know you can help.
- Care to tell them (sometimes with the most utmost candor) how your service can help them realize their objectives.
- Care to inform them what will happen to them if they don't take action to solve their problem.
- Care to understand their worries and anxieties both about what you are selling and about you.
- Care to make sure that you address these worries and anxieties-and not treat them as inconsequential.

- Care to be flexible in how you do business and when you do business so that your client understands that you are genuinely interested in their comfort and ease.
- In short, empathize. **Put yourself in your client's shoes and run your marketing- and write your cash copy- from their perspective, not from yours."**

This last point turns everything upside down in some investigator's minds. You have a need, a burning need, to tell the prospect how great you or your company is. You have a need, a burning need, to impress them; how your firm and only your firm can meet their needs.

It takes practice, but you can change the direction of your marketing copy and in your conversations, become a good listener first before you steer the discussion with probing questions. Only then can you begin to address their problems with your solutions.

Interest

Okay, you have the prospect's attention. However, Interest is a double-edged sword. On one side, they want to move forward; on the other hand, they have objections.

How do you make it easy for them to move forward?

- Make it easy to contact you with website forms and a google voice number. (Bonus: Every time you see your Google number on your phone display, you know it's a prospect.)
- Answer your calls with, "Hi, This is (Your full name). How can I help you?" "Is this Blazing Arrow Investigations?" "Yes it is, and whom am I speaking with?" * I call investigators all over the country to give them high-paying and interesting work. I can't tell you how many times I get the phone company's generic default answer, 'Leave a message,' a terse response, "Adamchilski, who's this?" or worse.

- Ease of discussion via a free consultation. Active listening sometimes calls for empathy and restating the problem in a way that makes sense for you and gives them a chance to agree or clarify the problem.
- Give them room to describe their problem to you by making sure your contact form has a text field that allows for a paragraph or two.
- FAQ - This is to pre-empt objections. Your FAQ, either on your website or woven into your discussion, is meant to overcome objections before they are raised and solidified in the prospect's mind.

It bears repeating, become a problem solver. Once you identify the problem, you can offer a specific solution for the pain point. By doing so, you are building:

Desire

That's right. Desire for a Private Investigator to address the problem and give the promise of a better future.

You are the expert; you have handled cases like this before. Hopefully, you can point to the testimonials on your website or collateral to show this. Because you are an expert, you have seen many variations of this problem and have a track record of being adaptable to each specific case.

Restate the prospect's painful situation, how your solution will apply, and how they will feel when the case is completed.

But first they must take:

SECTION FIVE: GUESS WHAT? YOU ARE ALWAYS CLOSING

Action

The prospect wants to move towards acting. Why? Why will they part with money for your solution? How will they do that?

What follows is an example argument you might make in favor of your services.

"Mrs. Gabbagottio, You need to know what is really going on. You can't live a life filled with his lies and deceit. You can't change the past, but with the information gleaned from our investigation, you can move forward with confidence. You won't be guessing anymore. Yes, it will be painful knowing the truth, if it is what you suspect it is, but at least you will know, and then you can decide how and when to act based on the information we will supply."

"I just pulled up his DMV record and see that he drives a BMW 7 series, black in color, is that correct? Which of the social media pictures here is the most recent? You said you suspect the activity will take place when you go to your sister's house out of state this coming weekend. I want to suggest coverage from the last time you see Mr. Gabbagottio until a few hours before your return, or we will begin tracking him after work if that makes more sense? We will stay with him until we know what he is doing and can address your concerns. Our price range on the refundable retainer, with some conditions for this work, is between $x and $z. We need you to fill out the retainer agreement here, and here, and initial here on the conditions."

"Once I confirm the payment from you, we will be all set."

"Will that be by credit card or PayPal?"

(Or whichever digital transfer methods you accept)

"Yes, we do take cash. I can give you a receipt. Let's set this up now."

Pushy? This is a condensed version of what may take place over several conversations.

A.I.D.A

Direct? Yes. Problem, solution, contract, and payment follow a straight-line progression.

Professional? You are not a therapist, but you can be sympathetic. Is your solution the best alternative of several discussed? The action steps should be the logical and **ethical** response to the issue the client is facing.

In a B2C interaction, you are the professional, and they are the sometimes-emotional amateur. Your professionalism includes the ethical obligation to do right by your client; not to inflame their passions so that you can empty their checkbook.

In a B2B sale, you are continually circling back to make sure you have agreement on solutions, and by the time the ACTION step arrives, the client is ready to move forward. The money part is just the housekeeping both sides know has to be done between you and the ultimate purchaser of your services.

In a P2P sale, you are looking to confirm that you and the client have brainstormed the issues and cobbled together the best approach. Your quote comes after you can see the complete picture of your investigative objective. You might have to offer a discount for a first-time client, but you must be firm it is only a one-time offer so they can see how well your firm performs.

Note: I learned early to offer a volume discount only after the volume is established, not before. Action is a natural by-product once the desire to move on the issue with your collective solution is hammered out.

SECTION FIVE: GUESS WHAT? YOU ARE ALWAYS CLOSING

SELLING STEPS

What we are about to talk about is **your** activity during the sales process.

Opening, Qualify

Do you have their **attention**? Is your firm a good fit? Remember, you can refer them to another colleague if appropriate. You can also use the consultation time to help them understand they should skip GO, save the $200 or $2,000, and go right to an attorney or another solution provider. The opening is not about taking all comers. You need to understand their wants, needs, or fears.

Part of qualifying the prospect is establishing rapport. Here you have a leg up on most salespeople. You know how to establish rapport and make people feel at ease when they talk with you. If you can ethically convince someone to make a statement against their own interest, you can certainly speak to somebody about their needs and wants. What you have learned from your street work applies here. Frame the issue and get on their wavelength. Salespeople tend to rush this step and fly headlong into their sales pitch.

Get the prospect talking and relaxing into what they want to talk about. This is not the time to tell them how wonderful your firm is and how you can meet their needs. You are a sympathetic listener.

Interviewing/Information Gathering

This step is often brushed over in a hurry to get the sale. Undoubtedly try to understand the investigative objective. This should keep the prospect's **interest**.

If you see them fading, you may have to touch upon their wants, needs, or fears. Their ideas of what a PI can do may be informed by Hollywood, far from the legal or ethical rules we are bound by.

You need to adjust expectations to rebuild their **interest**. This is where you spend the most time in this four-step process. As a trained investigator, you are trying to understand their motives for wanting to utilize a PI's services, as well as establish the parameters of the case.

Imagine the most under-utilized step by salespeople is the most crucial step and as an investigator, **you** have the skill sets to do it well.

Presentation

By this stage, you have gathered enough information from the prospect from conversations, emails, or texts and can put together a presentation.

If you are not creating a **desire** during your presentation for the expert solution you have crafted for them, you have to go back and restate why they are qualified, summarize the information you gathered, and present your solution with the hoped-for outcome clearly defined.

You may have to overcome objections with a restatement of how the answer will bring about the desired result.

Close

You want the prospect to take **Action**. You qualified them after you got their **attention**, and you kept their **interest** up while you gather information about their wants, needs, or fears.

This is different from picking the Who, What, How, When, Where, and Why of the case.

You made your presentation and see that they **desire** the outcome your services will provide. Here is how you close. Wrap everything up with:

"Makes sense to me. What do you think?"

That's a winning close that I must credit to Stephan Schiffman! I will recommend his books at the end of the chapter. I recommend you read his tips to help take the fear and loathing out of the sales cycle.

John's Example

In early June, a few years back, John was standing at his exhibit booth long after all the other vendors had packed up and headed out for happy hour. This was his first booth exhibition at this particular day-long Bar Association meeting, and he was determined to get his money's worth. John was waiting for the last class to end. The lawyers were getting their CLE credit certificates handed to them at the end of the class, so they all had to stay until the end.

Since John was the last man standing when the doors opened from the class, he decided to hand each attendee his brochure personally, price sheet and business card all nicely paper clipped together. One lawyer lagged behind and read the materials while John finished giving a package to each attorney. John's messaging was consistent. The lawyer didn't say what the case was about, but that he would reach out to John when the time was right.

Six months later, the right time was the Monday, three days before Christmas. John received a call from the attorney who explained that the VP of a Financing company had an urgent case for him. John called the VP, and they met on Christmas Eve at 10 AM.

The financing company had a problem. A big problem. Their inventory practices were somewhat lax and preliminary indications were that much of the heavy equipment they had financed for a safety company providing services and equipment to the Oil & Gas Fracking industry had gone missing when the price of oil dropped to the point where further exploration was no longer cost-effective. Some of the equipment had been abandoned on the job sites as the market collapsed.

The partners of that safety firm were hemorrhaging cash and pointing fingers at each other, and at the General Manager who was not cooperating.

The VP wanted a solution in place before he started his year-end vacation.

The missing equipment had last been seen at job sites in West Virginia, Kentucky, and Ohio.

This is what John knew before he walked into the high class, well-appointed offices of the VP. Framed photos of the veep and his bride in Aruba became the ice-breaker. John and his wife wanted to vacation there, and he asked about it. The VP asked John how he took his coffee as he served him from a fresh pot on the credenza. He then thanked John for coming in on short notice and Christmas Eve, no less. Their offices would be closing at noon. John realized neither the VP nor his attorney had envisioned the scope of the problem. Criminal prosecution, Civil Fraud, and Restitution were all in play, but they had not yet gotten an accurate inventory from all the players. They were stymied. The previous year's inventory, supposedly done by a third-party vendor, was questionable.

John had a blank slate to work with, but not a blank check. The more probing John did, the more interested the VP became in brainstorming a solution. Long after his staff wished the VP happy holidays and the outer offices darkened, John and VP hammered out a two-step approach to investigative steps. Talk to the players first, then go out into the field and see what the locals and ex-employees had to say.

Every 40 hours of billable work, John would hand-deliver his reports and pick up a new retainer. During the presentation phase, John walked the VP through AIDA with his opening, qualifying, information gathering, and negotiation. A three-hour meeting closed with the VP pulling out the checkbook and handing John a five-figure retainer check.

After, John enjoyed a pleasant sleigh ride home, humming along to Burl Ives singing his signature Christmas song.

Resources

Three books I recommend for this section are readable, actionable, and will give you clear direction in your five weekly sales and marketing hours, of how to call and meet prospects by appointment. They are all written by Stephan Schiffman and can be found on Amazon:

Cold Calling Techniques (That Really Work!)

Closing Techniques (That Really Work!)

Upselling Techniques (That Really Work!)

For an investigator who would rather have taken the trash out than pick up the phone and market, these books saved my business. Really!

Does it seem redundant to overlay these four steps on top of AIDA? You might say yes, but here is the crucial difference. AIDA is all about the prospect's reactions, questions, behaviors and their movement in making a decision. AIDA is all about the **prospect** while Selling is all about **your** workflow.

SECTION SIX:
WHEN YOU ARE A HAMMER, YOU ARE ALWAYS IN SEARCH OF NAILS

IN SEARCH OF NAILS

The best example of this is Truth Be Told Investigations, Inc.

Beth Clark provides surveillance solutions to consumers, mostly for Infidelity Investigations. Now she is getting inquiries from the law firms who represent her upscale clients.

Those very happy lawyers tell their partners that represent insurance companies, governmental entities, and major corporations about Beth's outstanding results.

Those attorneys now want Beth to hammer on their cases. They pay a little more per case, and the lure is, where the consumer may approach her once or twice and make the occasional referral, insurance companies are steady clients.

At any given time, a litigation supervisor will have hundreds of cases on their desk where surveillance may be a useful tool in determining if a person is as hurt as they say they are.

Beth has to jump through hoops to get paid as the users (the attorneys) are not the buyers (claims adjusters), and the buyers are buried in paperwork and make payments when they get around to them.

SECTION SIX: WHEN YOU ARE A HAMMER, YOU ARE ALWAYS IN SEARCH OF NAILS

It is hurting cash flow, and she has to spend time chasing receivables. Hate to say it, but insurance companies view surveillance services as a commodity, and no one vendor is irreplaceable. They dictate pricing and decide if they will pay for travel time, mileage, and pre-surveillance database work-ups.

With the consumers, she gets paid up front. The consumer is usually the buyer and user of the information whereas attorneys are the users, but claims adjustors are the buyers.

The consumer cases are mostly night and weekends while the insurance companies like to see what the claimant is doing on the weekend as well. Beth and Mary are torn between two masters.

It's a no-brainer to prioritize the clients who give them tons of cases, but the people in Beth's B2C market suffer.

By working for the insurance companies, her responsiveness and quality suffer with her target audience.

Then a wealthy school district calls her. They seem to have many students matriculating who may not live within the school district. They want Beth to find out where the kids really live.

Not long after, the lawyer for a neighboring town contacts Beth to follow employees whom they suspect of working on side businesses while clocked in on the town's time.

In both cases, a bidding process must be completed, and purchase orders filled out. The reporting requirements are far different from what she supplies the consumer client or insurance client. They have restrictions on report and travel time, and they want to cap mileage. In both cases, she gets into a bidding war with a retired cop who had once been the preferred vendor. She has to bow out.

> Instead, what if Beth resisted the sirens' call of the repeat customer, with all their issues, and concentrated on offering more services to her target audience?
>
> Instead of going so wide outside of her nets, what if she goes deeper?

Already, she is receiving requests from the soon-to-be-divorced clients to find assets the errant spouse was hiding.

Then there are the pre-marital background checks. The wealthy parents are sure that Mister or Miss Right is wrong for their misguided and love-struck child.

Sam or Sally ask Beth to find their long-lost black-sheep sibling to attempt to make amends.

The skill sets necessary for Beth to meet her own high standards are similar to those she picked up doing Intelligence in the Army. Beth services the same target audience better with premium products and services. The testimonials and referrals are coming from consumers, not school superintendents or town supervisors.

What I Learned From The Parachute

What Color is my Parachute, updated annually by Richard Bolles, is a book geared to job hunters and career changers. The author has both a growing and recurring market. I often recommend this book to people who get blindsided in a lay-off or an unjust firing. He helps them dust themselves off and provides the tools to make their new job **getting** a job.

One of the things that attracted me to his writing, and to refer his book to you, is the information regarding transferable skill sets.

SECTION SIX: WHEN YOU ARE A HAMMER, YOU ARE ALWAYS IN SEARCH OF NAILS

Think of a person like Tony Russo, who was a cop and a detective for most of his career. When you look at him, you see a person with an unusual occupation.

He might look at going out on his own through a more narrow lens. *What do I know about sales, marketing, and accounting?*

Yet his squad worked on enough economic crime cases to understand how thefts or frauds were perpetrated and find the evidence of the wrongdoing to make an arrest that stuck.

If he could understand the intricacies of economic crimes, he can follow the basic tenets of accounting.

If he could interview witnesses, persons of interest, and suspects, he could certainly learn about AIDA and the four steps of selling.

Many people who worked in the same job, doing the same type of work every day, might share that same narrow view about their skills.

Bolles uses checklists and questionnaires to tease out complimentary skills and widen their scope to see that they can do more than they initially thought.

Another resource is AARP's *Life Reimagined* tabs on their website. AARP realizes many retirees are healthy and still have much gas left in their tank. AARP sees these people need to do something different in their "second career."

AARP created a series of checklist and questionnaires to help retirees decide what they want to do while they are still healthy enough to do it.

If you have behaved, so far, like a hammer always looking for nails, transferrable skills are the other tools in your toolbox. Don't try to hammer everything. Explore what other tools (skill sets) you can use to serve your target audience.

The most transferrable skill for Tony to aid his expanding Target Audience is Criminal Defense Investigation. However, even here, Tony understands he has to sharpen his tools.

In quick order, he purchased Brandon Perron's *Uncovering Reasonable Doubt: The Component Method*.

He found the National Association of Public Defenders (NAPD) webinars compiled expertly by Jeff Sherr.

On the advice of his attorney friend, he became a member of the National Association of Criminal Defense Lawyers (NACDL).

To work civil financial cases, he joined the Association of Certified Fraud Examiners (ACFE) and planned to become a Certified Fraud Examiner.

He joined the New York PI Association, ALDONYS.

SECTION SIX: WHEN YOU ARE A HAMMER, YOU ARE ALWAYS IN SEARCH OF NAILS

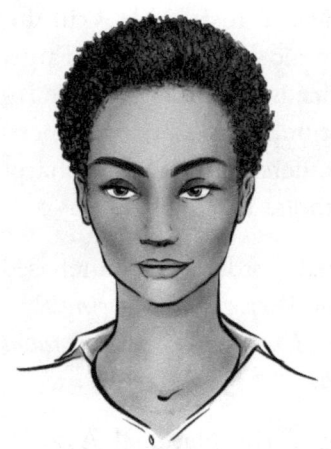

Open Source Intelligence (OSINT) investigation has captured Beth's passion. Right now, surveillance is paying the bills, but more and more consumers and Austin's high-end law firms are requesting her OSINT services.

She can charge a premium and has made it a "paying hobby" within her business.

Even as a start-up, Beth has a paying hobby now that the Armored Guard days are behind her. She attends the OSMOSIS conference, put on by Cynthia Hetherington in Las Vegas in the fall, and will be attending TALI's annual conference as well.

His target audience was Property and Casualty Insurance Companies.

Surveillance was not even on the radar when John started Independent Special's Investigations but slowly became a money-maker. Claims adjusters that requested insurance fraud investigations also required surveillance. It was a complementary offering and so specialized that he hired surveillance operatives whom he cross-trained to become investigators.

His margins were lower for surveillance, but it allowed him to keep his growing staff employed full-time.

The Casualty Adjusters also requested that John find witnesses and take their statements. He charged his investigative rates as opposed to the lower prices charged by Independent Adjustors.

He created attractive flat rates for Accident Scene Photography and Measurements. He performed other complex investigations for his target audience and met their needs with his specialized insurance knowledge.

As long as they were willing to pay his rates, he was willing to do the work. Teaching his people how to do casualty investigations was more straightforward for John than teaching fraud principles.

These high times were about to come to an end, but he didn't yet see what was on the other side of the clouds.

SECTION SIX: WHEN YOU ARE A HAMMER, YOU ARE ALWAYS IN SEARCH OF NAILS

I Don't Do That!

> How many times does a customer in your target market have to ask for a service you decline to perform before you will sit up and listen?

As long as it is not unethical, illegal, or immoral, you better have some clear reasons why not.

If it's not in your proverbial wheelhouse, and you feel uncomfortable saying yes to a task that you may fail at, you must receive the umpteenth request with a more open mind.

You can always refuse a prospect that asks for bargain-basement pricing; you can refuse to go to farthest edge of your geographic reach on short notice; and you can refuse to handle a case on a holiday weekend (but you can also refer them to them to other investigators and take a 20% commission off the top line for the trouble).

However, multiple reasonable requests for a skill you don't yet have should be a signal that it's time to expand your skill set.

You get a call from one of your best clients. It is the Wednesday before the four-day Labor Day Weekend. They want you to do around-the-clock surveillance in East Bumrush?

"I'll check on my availability and get back to you," you say.

You contact your buddy in West Bumrush and sell it to them at your rates, minus your 20%. They are happy to do it, and you get paid when they get paid. You call the client back and tell them the bad news first. You can't do it, but your good friend and business associate from West Bumrush is standing by to take on the assignment, and you would be more than happy to make the introduction. Best of all, since the client is a great client, you won't charge a rush premium. The client is doubly grateful.

If you have been turning down work from your target audience because you lack the skill set, what if you learn the skill so you can charge your regular rates for it, or even a premium?

If the work doesn't bore the living bejesus out of you, what is holding you back?

The services performed will help your target market—the exact people you are sending your message to. They might be using you regularly, but if you don't add this service to your offering, you are telling them to look elsewhere for a solution. Better you look elsewhere for them, vet a provider, and present your client with the answer.

Why do you really turn down work?

Richard Dawson's Family Feud Survey says:

- "I don't do that type of work."
- "Fear of failure." (But you never say that you make up some other BS excuse.)
- "It will take too long, and it will take too long to get paid."
- "I can't do it on such short notice."

Maybe you could turn those reasons around and see the opportunity for what it really is, a chance to learn something new and to try something new. Maybe, just maybe, you might like doing something different for a change, instead of the same old, same old.

Maybe you can learn something about this case you can apply to all your clientele. But...

Beware BSO - Bright Shiny Objects (AKA Magic Bullets)

Maybe I am more entrepreneurial than some. I have tested a dozen proof of concepts over the years to see if they could sustain a business or a side business. I am not bashful about talking about any of them and the education that came from those experiences.

I once spent a summer's worth of Wednesdays and Fridays, and $46,000, with a team of really smart techies to unlock the secrets of connecting people to billions of dollars sitting in unclaimed matured savings bonds collecting dust in the US Treasury. Talk about a BSO.

In the end, we could not make it replicable or scalable. I worked long hours the other days of the week, and Saturday, to keep my company afloat while I tested this concept.

Do I have any regrets? Heck no. I learned more about data-mining in that summer than I would have in a college program, and every Friday we all went to a different Ice Cream store at the end of the day. I am still friends with the team.

What does that have to do with a Private Investigation Business, you ask. I joined a team asked to locate and talk to family members of a dead person whose Savings Bonds were not even collecting interest any longer. Getting good phone numbers for them was the most significant challenge as landlines were going dead every day, and mobile numbers were not yet showing up in the databases. We then had to establish rapport with the family members, interview them, and determine if they were the closest family of the decedent. It forced us to find different ways to locate people. From that summer, I was able to create a flat rate for Locates that I still sell every day.

Beware the single case that effectively shuts down your business for over thirty days and places your customers in second place. The customers will go elsewhere.

Beware the new customer that starts giving you plenty of cases but hasn't paid you for the first one yet. If they have that kind of volume, they were using somebody before you. Is this client a "burner" or will they grind you to give them a discount after the work is performed?

Beware servicing a customer outside your target audience at a lower profit margin. Would you be better off using that time to market your higher-priced offerings to your target audience?

Beware sub-contracting for less than 75% of your regular rate. I restrict my marketing costs to procure a new customer at 20% of my billable hour, so subbing at 80% of regular rates is okay. Anything less would eat into the profit margin.

Beware the case that jeopardizes your license, livelihood, or life. You must walk away when you realize what's going on.

Beth's Side Hustle

Beth loved doing intelligence gathering and analysis in the sandbox of Afghanistan. She did two tours but had enough of the spartan army life.

After her launch of Truth Be Told Investigations, Inc., she is surprised to find so many different customer segments clamoring for her to gather intelligence. Whether it's on an errant spouse, a prospective spouse, or players in a big merger and acquisition deal, she loves the work.

When she doesn't have the eyeball on two-car surveillance with Mary, she whips out her laptop with a stable internet connection and gets lost in the data.

Somebody else might have pulled out a book or binge-watched YouTube videos, but not Beth. The importance of these OSINT cases dictates her fees.

Her upscale clients asked her to gather intelligence and told their friends Beth is a magician.

Almost from the beginning of her business, she tracks the time and money she is making on this side hustle. She spends half the time and charges twice or three times as much as she does for flat rates and budgeted cases. Beth uses it as an effective upsell after a successful outcome on her core business.

She devotes a page to her website just for OSINT, and the testimonials are rolling in. Her marketing of OSINT is purely organic.

What if she applies a mixture of inbound and outbound techniques to OSINT as she does for Truth Be Told?

SECTION SIX: WHEN YOU ARE A HAMMER, YOU ARE ALWAYS IN SEARCH OF NAILS

SUMMARY

Focus on all of your target market's needs, not just what you are best at. There are things you can learn and should learn, so you don't leave money on the table or worse.

Don't let your hard-earned clients go to another provider, who may have weaker skill sets than you but who isn't as rigid.

Avoid spreading your services outside your target market and instead drill deeper into your market with higher-margin offerings. If you specialize in Insurance Surveillance, it sounds counter-intuitive not to work an Infidelity case or vice versa but in the long run, working outside your target market dissipates your energy or focus. Of course, that is the object if you are working on your marketing. If you are not working on your marketing, and are taking all comers when the work dries up you have no pipeline. All you have is a scattered customer base that direct marketing cannot effectively engage.

Beware Bright Shiny Objects. They will derail you from your well thought out business and marketing plans. If you do engage in them, treat them like a paying hobby and do not let them detract from your business focus.

SECTION SEVEN:
YOU CAN MARKET LESS THAN 5 HOURS A WEEK. REALLY!

WHY LESS THAN 5 HOURS A WEEK?

Because it is more than zero hours a week and implements a steady approach. You own your Private Investigation Business and marketing is part of your job now. Spending less than 5 hours a week marketing doesn't feel like Sisyphus pushing the boulder up the hill every day of eternity.

Five hours is 16% of a 40-hour week (and that is a short week for small-business owners).

5 out of 50 is 10%, 5 out of 55 is 9%.

Can you spend between 9 and 16% of your work week feeding your PI business?

Most PIs say yes, but the rub is not the time commitment, it is **how** to market.

How do you get started? Where do you start? How do you get your butt in the chair and do the work?

You have heard the saying many times: "Plan the work and work the plan."

The PI that markets:

- Has a SMART marketing plan— something they can pick up on Monday morning and get back to it.
- Has a CRM with leads in the pipeline that make it easy to start the week off.
- Knows marketing hours includes cold calls, appointments, fixing broken links on the website, warm-calling clients for referrals and introductions, gathering testimonials, and emailing prospects that downloaded your free checklist, free report, or e-Book.
- Walks a prospect through their sales funnel. By now, they know the acronym AIDA and how it works with the sales process of Introduction/Qualifying/Information Gathering/Presentation/Closing. Bonus: selling counts as marketing time.
- Attends Seminars, Conferences, monthly, quarterly, and yearly association meetings where they are the vendor or attendee with a marketing agenda.

The above are necessary marketing hours. SEO optimization and attracting leads to your website are a little more advanced, but can be learned and implemented, and will especially help if you are in the B2C world. I would tend to categorize time with your IT people or working on the website for B2C as admin time. Harvesting the leads your website gathers and nurturing them would count towards marketing time.

Tony's Five

Tony visits a leads groups meeting at the Chamber of Commerce every other Wednesday for an hour and a half, and a BNI every Thursday for two hours. These are face-to-face meetings with professionals he wants to connect with.

He also tries to schedule early morning hour-long appointments with qualified prospects for Thursdays and Fridays. He uses his association lists to call CPAs and business lawyers for an hour each day on Mondays and Tuesdays. He is getting better at getting call-backs as he tweaks his call scripts. He fields call-backs and enters all the data into the CRM on his laptop as it occurs.

Tony attends monthly Bar Association after-hour events and meets his clients there. He has them introduce him to other attorneys they are talking to. It usually results in a warm introduction and testimonial.

Boy, those Wildebeests like to drink.

Since the big murder case in Nassau County, he fields calls from Criminal Defense attorneys with cases there. He counts his free consultation with them as part of the marketing and sales time involved in qualifying the prospect's case.

Tony's marketing time sometimes creeps up to 10 hours a week, but he has a plan that has him marketing at least 4.75 hours a week.

Beth's Five

The live chat function on her website has her and Mary Chambers, her employee, fielding inquiries and qualifying prospects at least seven total hours a week. She hires and trains a new Administrative Assistant, Pat, to cover calls from 5 pm to 9 pm, when most of the calls come in. Beth finds that Pat converts a higher number of cases to hourly cases which pay better than the flat rates. Beth trains two new operatives to work the hourly and 8-hour flat rate surveillance cases. Pat becomes adept at scheduling the field assignments. Mary fields the daytime callers while working 4-hour flat rate jobs and the more natural background checks. Beth qualifies the prospects that make email inquiries.

Inbound marketing is clearly exceeding 5 hours a week

Beth, Mary, and Pat are working on their sales scripts to increase conversions, but quickly realize their niche has a lot of tire-kickers and persons who would instead not find out what is really going on when their loved one goes out for milk and comes back two hours with bread.

Beth's inbound marketing is automated, and the team is engaged in sales.

Beth continues outbound marketing with leads groups and visits where her upscale wildebeests figuratively drink.

She visits upscale hair salons, beauty and nail salons, wellness studios, and gyms in a twenty-five-mile radius of downtown Austin, Texas. She offers the workers a deep discount on flat rates, and they send referrals to Beth from their client base. The owners of those facilities and their workers split a commission that Beth pays. Everybody is happy.

Beth stops by these providers on her way out to her working cases and makes her marketing pitch. She does this less than five hours a week.

The results she gets for her upscale clients attract the attention of her clients' high-end lawyers. She drives some of the video and reports into the law firms and meets other lawyers in the firm. They ask if she can do different kinds of background checks, including due diligence. She takes on Bodily Injury and Workers compensation cases for these lawyers as well but finds the insurance company vendor requirements and commodity pricing off-putting.

Even though the lawyer is doing the hiring, they are passing Beth's bills to out of state claims departments. She experiences heartburn from trying to collect on past due bills. She is reminded that her user is not her buyer.

What is most surprising to Beth is the variety of uses for her OSINT (Open Source Intelligence). The law firms are her most prominent clients, followed by her upscale clients. This is all organic marketing, and when she sees the per-case profit-margins, she wonders why they are grinding out tons of B2C surveillance hours every day.

John's Five

Each newsletter took about 4 hours to create before he gave it to his secretary for mailing. The training classes were usually 4 to 6 hours, depending on whether John brought in Pizza and Salads for a working lunch. Many of the clients were out of state, so he made a marketing swing: AIG in Albany, Utica National in Utica, Peerless and National Grange in Syracuse, and Merchants Mutual in Buffalo before making the long trek home.

Training was a quarterly event. When he was in office, he filled out the mornings phoning new claims adjusters to chat, then followed up by sending them his brochures and price sheets.

In the two-plus years of servicing a loyal clientele, he found out claims adjusters move between jobs all the time and were his best evangelists with their new employers.

John leveraged this movement by meeting the new company's Claims supervisors, SIU, and Claims Managers. Free introductory cases and price-matching worked to dislodge their present contract investigators who had fallen asleep at the switch.

He used ACT to keep a record of his leads, prospects, customers, and clients. With B2B, he had lower margins on the surveillance work and his flat rates—which didn't allow him to charge for travel expense and time—weren't making up the difference.

Revenues were up, but so were expenses. His profit margin fell from 47% in year one to 31% in year three. Some of that had to do with 10% increases in salaries every year (the nationwide average is 5-6%). He implemented a bonus plan based on revenue and quality control goals.

He established contacts with Insurance Defense Law Firms but couldn't charge a premium on their most critical high-dollar cases. He did not market the law firms for their other types of cases and stayed focused on working for the insurance companies that hire the lawyers. He turned down Infidelity investigations and the occasional Personal Injury cases handled by those dyed-in-the-wool Defense firms.

He increased his pricing every year, but could not charge premiums for any of his services. Things were good, and he stuck to the knitting, as the saying goes.

John expanded his fraud investigation work with large and small insurance carriers, as well as third-party administrators. He sought licenses in New Jersey, New Hampshire, and Maine as part of his "Bangor to Baltimore" coverage.

Your Five

How you craft your five hours per week depends on your SMART marketing plan which is built upon your:

- Business Segmentation–B2C, B2C, P2P, Hybrid Specialist, Hybrid by Geography
- Target Audience–Claims Departments, Attorneys, Professionals, Corporate-Government-NGO, CPAs, Small Businesses, Landlords/Property Managers, Individuals, Other Private Investigators
- Brand–Range of Services
- Marketing Copy or Marketing Message
- Inbound/Outbound methods
- CRM and Email Capture
- Attendance at gatherings, meetings, and conferences
- Email, Phone, and Presentation scripts (Schiffman books are recommended)

Go into your marketing time knowing that you will have periods of discomfort. No baby started walking without falling down a bunch of times.

Tip: Set a timer for a 55-minute marketing session and don't get distracted until the timer goes off.

You may encounter reasonable situations that prevent you from marketing at your scheduled time. Immediately schedule a make-up time for the same day.

There will be times when a whole week goes by while you have done zero marketing. If you are keeping score and can see those zeros staring at you, you will be motivated to get up off the ground and try putting one foot in front of the other again.

If the pattern of avoidance persists after you have made an effort to create a viable marketing plan, you have no one to blame for the empty pipeline other than the person staring at you in the mirror. That sounds harsh, but rather than skip blindly along in the dark, think about why you are resistant to marketing. Is it the methods that you have chosen?

Were there some marketing activities you enjoyed more than others? Can you double up on them?

Do you have trouble getting the phone call or emailing engine started? Try calling a good customer you haven't talked to in a while. Then call another and then another. Count those calls as marketing calls and after you warm up with friendly voices, plunge into the cold calling.

Pull your calendar out and block off the first hour and a half of your business day every Monday-Thursday (except for the days where you have bonafide marketing appointments). Example: 8:30-9:30 am, Monday-Thursday.

What activity is the best use of your marketing time for that period? Is it cold-calling, warm-calling, or asking for testimonials and referrals? Is it creating free content for the website? Training for your target audience? Is it returning calls or emails to qualify prospects?

Set the timer and go for it.

Are you adding leads, prospects, and new customers into your CRM? Are you tracking how the leads come in?

How are you tracking conversions?

- Converting leads to prospects
- Converting prospects to customers
- Up-selling the right service at the right time for the right client.
- Converting customers into referral-generators or testimonial-givers.

SECTION SEVEN: YOU CAN MARKET LESS THAN 5 HOURS A WEEK. REALLY

Work your marketing plan. There are no shortcuts. It does get easier. With repetition, you will become more relaxed as see how your plan works.

SECTION EIGHT: FLYING FORTRESS

CONSIDER THE B-17

I understand why you might be resistant to change. I was there myself in the face of some pretty steep adversity.

Consider the B-17 Flying Fortress, an American heavy bomber deployed in WWII. It flew missions in both theaters of conflict. Most of this bomber's acclaim came from dangerous daylight bombing missions over Germany and Occupied France, without the benefit of fighter escort.

The bomber groups were alone in the sky, facing radar-assisted anti-aircraft guns, and defending themselves against swarms of enemy fighter aircraft.

TV shows such as *12 O'Clock High* and the Movie Memphis Belle added to the bomber's legacy as a warbird that could take incredible punishment and still bring its 10-men crews back to safety in England. If forced, it could fly on only two of its four engines.

In February of 2001, my figurative B-17, the high-flying Independent Special Investigations, LLC, was crippled by two blows.

Two national Private Investigation companies disrupted the Property and Casualty Insurance Industry with a well-funded marketing plan. "Disruption" is the proper word. Here is how they did it.

Where I marketed to local offices, they went to the Home Offices with two promises. They could take assignments anywhere in the country through one single 800 number, and then the assigning claims adjusters could watch the progress of their cases in a simple dashboard.

800 numbers were common at the time, but nationwide service coupled with the online dashboards was not. This was cutting edge. Think of how 1-800-Flowers disrupted FTD's stranglehold on ordering flowers.

Local branches of the XYZ and ABC insurance companies made up over 55% of my business. Then these competitors asked the Home Offices for—and received—one- or two-year contracts with the **entire** claims department of the XYZ insurance company and the ABC company, among other insurance companies. None of the local PI's were working with contracts.

Within 60 days, the time it would take to work out my present backlog on their files, I would be flying a heavy bomber with only two working engines. It was a long way back to the white cliffs of Dover.

What added insult to injury, those two companies tried to hire my crew and me for about 30% of our billable hour rate to service our own customers, who were forced by their home office to use the national competitor.

My customers were not happy and apologized to me but their hands, or more appropriately their purse strings, were tied. I quickly learned the difference between the user and the ultimate buyer. The Claims VP held the purse strings and wrestled back autonomy over the SIU units. Sadly, those national competitors were now eating my lunch and were charging more per hour than I was in my own backyard.

A month into this debacle, I went to a meeting in Phoenix and met with other similarly-affected PIs. Their shell-shocked faces told the same story. We realized we had all been watching the white fluffy clouds without any contingency plans for the trouble brewing on the horizon.

Most, if not all, of our incomes, came from one source, and that was local claim departments. This was a disruption, not just a faster, better and cheaper competitor. McDonald's was not moving next to Burger King. This was like what Uber and Lyft are doing to the taxi business.

One PI at the meeting was immune from this disruption. I met him a few times before and knew he had a successful company in the Windy City, Chicago. He was the go-to guy in Chicago for just about everything. It was his primary business to service the legal community. He had expanded to take on the newly created SIU work, but he wasn't entirely dependent on it. He supervised a group of highly skilled investigators and invested in office staff and a contract internet librarian.

I considered myself an expert in Insurance Fraud and not a generalist. In our earlier encounters, I wished him well.

Now, he was like a guru to the half of the group that wanted to survive (the other half went to the bar to drown their sorrows). My people were not going to drown in the English Channel, and I was going to bring my airship home.

First, I had to get over my attitude towards other Private Investigators. I had been with an SIU, and now I was Independent Special Investigations. That costly PI license didn't mean much other than allowing me to do privately what I had once done as a salaried employee, but I still resisted making the mindset changes.

I had to learn how to market. In all honesty, to that point, all I had done was copy my company employee mindset methods for gaining and retaining internal customers. The newsletter and training worked well for adjusters, but what if that spigot got shut off? Still, I resisted looking for other types of business such as lawyers or private individuals.

I was losing altitude and could run out of money, and still, I didn't change my target audience, even though it was forever changed by a technology that was out of my reach at the time.

The Nationals were investing in programmers at the earliest time in the Internet. I was having a hard time hiring an administrative assistant. I could not compete, because I couldn't afford it. Family loans had bankrolled one. I didn't have an extra hundred thousand dollars laying around.

I doubled down on what I did best. Marketing time increased dramatically. I began reaching out to other smaller insurance carriers, specialty groups, and third-party administrators. I reach out to Self-Insureds. Oh, and those lawyers that handled Insurance defense claims as part of their broader business mix. I talked to them too.

I was partially effective with this reach, but keep in mind I was not skilled enough to effectively gauge their AIDA or my sales skills. I recall driving all the way to Southern Maine to talk to a Claims VP of a small carrier, only to find out they had little or no work in Southern New England and none in New York State.

My plane was losing altitude quickly as my checkbook was getting leaner and leaner. It was hard to let go of employees I trained in my work methods and company culture. I wasn't replacing revenue fast enough and had to lighten my load.

I waved goodbye to sub-contractors almost immediately, and my part-timers went back to their day jobs. Two employees went to law school. One chose to be a stay-at-home mom. My surveillance manager went to work in a non-competing position with his friend for a while, before changing careers entirely.

Since the remaining two employees and I had surveillance training, our plane was skimming above the treetops with surveillance jobs and the fraud cases, but full-time paychecks were not always the norm. I didn't cut wages, but the bonus plan was thrown out the bomb bay doors along with the annual conference training classes.

For a while, it seems that a scaled down version of ISI, and the lower altitude was less stressful on the two engines. Our third sputtering engine was getting stronger with cases from new clients. When I wasn't marketing, I was back on the street doing investigations and doing surveillance on weekends. We were leveling off and even climbing, but it was a grind.

We took on some work that was not particularly lucrative, but it did absorb overhead. That summer, I traveled to Eastern Massachusetts one night a week to help an SIU Director run off the remaining case files of his laid-off staff, as they outsourced new cases to the National competitor. It even made his job redundant. I was working him out of a job, but it seemed like we would survive to go into the fall of 2001.

One September morning, under crystal-clear blues skies, my first hire Jon and I were driving back from a weekend surveillance in Princeton, New Jersey. We were listening to Howard Stern when reports came into him that a plane had hit one of the twin towers. And then the second plane hit the other tower. Nobody knew what to think at first, but as videos of the crashes made their way onto network TV, Stern reported on what he saw.

We were on Route 1, heading towards New York City and, as we crested a rise, we saw smoke billowing from each tower towards Brooklyn. Where was Mike, my third hire? We couldn't get ahold of him. Finally, he got to a landline and called his wife to tell her that he was safe in Brooklyn, but that all the bridges were shut down. He would eventually get home that night.

Ourselves, we skirted the city. As we crossed the Tappan Zee Bridge over the Hudson and North of the city, we saw both towers had collapsed. Moreover, with that collapse went much of the work I built up over those six months. Insurance companies put the brakes on all spending.

Shortly after that, when the business paralysis that gripped the country began to loosen, we were able to resume operations.

The idea of the regional company (Bangor to Baltimore) evaporated when I went back on the street with only two employees. I was determined not to lay them off, but in the end, I could only keep one of them on. Luckily the second found a good job, thanks to the skills he learned from me and my glowing testimonial.

The following year, the remaining employee had accumulated four years of experience between ISI and the previous surveillance company, and created his own company, parachuting to safety over the English countryside.

I landed alone seven years, almost to the day, after taking off.

I owned my own business but was barely keeping out of the poorhouse. My revenues plummeted 80% from the high years to where I was scratching out about 26 billable hours a week by myself. The funny thing was, my overhead was pared down to the bone and my income improved. However, this was not my idea of a fun time. I had to stop blaming smarter, better-funded competitors.

I rebranded as Squire Investigations, determined to make it as a solo-generalist serving the legal community in Southern Connecticut.

I finally listened to my Chicago friend and took a page from his playbook!

I joined the National Association of Legal Investigators. There I found many Private Investigators, experts in their field, who were wholly dedicated to their craft and seemed to make a good living. I sat for and passed the rigorous testing to become a Certified Legal Investigator. Later, the association elected me their Regional Director.

I joined the Milford, Connecticut Chamber of Commerce where I met a business coach. He was offering a 12-week group class. I put the expense on an interest-free credit card and started learning about business and marketing. I took a day-long course put on by Jimmie Mesis, the former owner of PI Magazine, to learn affiliate marketing. I will mention more of Jimmie in *How To Boost Your Private Investigation Business Into Orbit: Make $1,000 Every Working Day!*

This is a story about almost crashing and burning. I am sharing this, so you understand I started my firm with few business and marketing skills. When faced with adversity, I didn't quit, but I also didn't learn everything I needed right away. I was stubbornly running faster on the hamster wheel, but not getting ahead.

Squire Investigations became the beginning of my metamorphosis from an investigator in business, to a business person providing investigative services.

That happened when I focused on learning how to market and sell those investigative services.

SECTION EIGHT: FLYING FORTRESS

CONCLUSION

Tony Russo is well-positioned with his Business clients and his Criminal Defense Lawyers. He understands that marketing is part of his business and works hard at it.

He has had some success, and some problems with the "associates" part of Russo & Associates and he has some crucial decisions to make about strategic growth and a possible a change to his end game.

SECTION EIGHT: FLYING FORTRESS

Beth Clark launched with a strong inbound marketing strategy and hit a home run right out of the box with her outbound marketing to upscale women in the greater Austin area. She moved gradually from a soft launch and added employees to fill specific needs as the business blossomed. She knew that she had to learn about business no differently than the new skill sets from her army training. She was open to change from the beginning and embraced it. Within a short period, she realized that she had both a specialized skill set and passion for OSINT.

Everything is going as planned, but she faces a decision of what to do with her OSINT side hustle. Does she stay in the B2C world, or pivot to B2B before she adds more employees? She had begun with the goal of building a business that her employees will run for her or one that she can sell to a competitor.

Truthfully, John didn't employ every strategy he learned, but the ones he did implement were tested and measured. Marketing less than 5 hours a week was born from the Squire Investigations rebranding and startup. He was determined not to make the same mistakes he made with ISI. He still had a few wonderful insurance customers from those days, but he learned. New skills, such as criminal defense and forensic genealogy. He learned everything he could about investigative interviewing and was much more adept at locating people, and he balanced this skill building with learning about sales and marketing.

Get out your planner, set the timer, and start putting your marketing plan together.

It doesn't have to be exactly perfect. You will test and measure as you go along. We started this book off with a simple adage. "The marketing you do is better than the marketing you should do, but don't."

I will finish it with another quote. An old homicide detective once told me, **"Ain't nothing to it, but to do it."**

Now go and do it.

To my mentors and coaches: Jimmie Mesis, Cliff Ennico, Stephan Schiffman, Tom Maier, Paul Lavoie, Brent Denkins, and Bill Fotsch

NEED MORE HELP?

If you are launching your business soon and have questions or you are having trouble getting your company off the ground, I am available for a FREE 30-minute consultation. Please go to the contact form at www.ThePICoach.com and schedule a phone call with me. It may be an easy fix.

Also

I only coach PIs and limit my time to just eight individual sessions a week so that I can concentrate on helping each client reach their goals and achieve a life/work balance. My personal experience with coaches has been fantastic. One coach helped me save my business with marketing advice. Every time I utilized the services of a coach, the cost of their advice was paid back many times over.

ABOUT JOHN A. HODA, CLI, CFE

John A. Hoda is a licensed private investigator, blogger, and podcaster. He coaches other PIs how to be successful at **ThePICoach.com**

He graduated in 1975 with a B.S. in Criminology from Indiana University of Pennsylvania.

He is a former police officer, insurance fraud investigator, and has run several PI businesses over three decades.

He has written numerous articles for PI Magazine and is the creator of the DVD: *The Ultimate Guide to Taking Statements*. His cases have headlined in the Philadelphia Inquirer and the New Haven Register. He sat on the board of the National Association of Legal Investigators and the CT Assoc of Licensed Private Investigators. He is a Certified Legal Investigator and a Certified Fraud Examiner.

SECTION EIGHT: FLYING FORTRESS

John also writes fiction and has been a lifetime athlete playing club soccer and playing/coaching semi-professional football.

His podcast audience at My Favorite Detective Stories is growing every day. John interviews past and present investigators about their specialties and teases out what it takes to make for a successful investigation. The entire podcast catalog can be found at **JohnHoda.com**

OTHER BOOKS BY JOHN A. HODA

Get your FREE *Mugshots: My Favorite Detective Stories* downloaded in your favorite format right to your inbox by going to-**JohnHoda.com.**

Come ride around the country with veteran investigator John A. Hoda as he searches for the truth. He has selected great stories from a forty-plus year career and keeps serving them up like free refills at the all-night diner.

Non-Fiction

How to Launch Your Private Investigation Business: 90 days to Lift Off!

How to Boost Your Private Investigation Business: Make $1,000 every Working Day!

How to Rocket Your Private Investigation Business: The Complete Series

SECTION EIGHT: FLYING FORTRESS

Fiction

Odessa on the Delaware: Introducing Marsha O'Shea

A Crime Thriller with a mystery twist set in Philadelphia pitting a Russian mob enforcer against a homeless Marine Corp veteran. FBI Agent Marsha O'Shea is drawn into the case with a secret pushing her to follow the clues, only to uncover a greater secret that may get her killed in the final showdown.

Phantasy Baseball: It's About A Second Chance.

A thirty-nine-year-old little league coach discovers he has a magical pitch and gets a one in a million chance to try out for his beloved Philadelphia Phillies. He is unprepared for the roller-coaster magic-carpet ride in the Big Leagues.

ACKNOWLEDGMENTS

Rekka Jay for Cover Design, Illustrations, Editing, Formatting, Layout, Patience and Forgiveness.

Joanna Penn of **TheCreativePenn.com** for the information and inspiration needed to tackle my first non-fiction project.

My advanced copy readers who saved my butt countless times: Luis Reyes, Ron Getner, Rich Robertson, Brandon Perron, Cynthia Hetherington, Brian Ritucci, Jayne McElfresh, Lisa Garcia, Kate Minchin, Burt Hodge, Tony Raymond, Paul Rubin

The **Written Word-Milford Writers Group** for their support and encouragement.

Thanks to all.

www.ingramcontent.com/pod-product-compliance
Lightning Source LLC
Chambersburg PA
CBHW030443300426
44112CB00009B/1143